THE NEW COMMUNITY

The New Community

Religious Life in an Era of Change

Gabriel Moran

HERDER AND HERDER

1970
HERDER AND HERDER NEW YORK
232 Madison Avenue, New York, N.Y. 10016

Nihil obstat: Leo J. Steady, Censor Librorum
Imprimatur: ✠ Robert F. Joyce, Bishop of Burlington
March 2, 1970

Contents

Preface

THIS book is an interim report on the change taking place in religious orders. It is a companion to my earlier co-authored book, *Experiences in Community*. As essays which extend the argument of that book, it is obviously not a complete "treatise on religious life." It is simply a small contribution to the thinking on a few aspects of that life.

Since this book, like the previous one, refers in large part to the life of the sister, I would have preferred to co-author it with a sister. I was not able to work out such an arrangement and so I am publishing this alone. However, I feel that the ideas of this book are co-authored by dozens if not hundreds of people. They are the many sisters and brothers with whom I have come into contact in recent years. Whatever the value of this book may be, its truth is biographical and not ideological. Many people are talking today about a "new community," but often without much feel for the experienced life of such a community. I do not consider myself an expert on all the areas touched by the question of new communities, nor do I have any desire to make religious orders my specialty of study. But there are many people still in religious orders or recently out of them who need a spokesman. I reluctantly assume this position because I see very few other people speaking in this vein. Teilhard de Chardin often spoke of the growth of a band of "spiritual expatriates," alienated from the church but unsatisfied by any other alternatives. Among people still in religious orders and those recently out of the orders, the number of such expatriates is legion.

I would like to thank the men in my own new community in downtown Manhattan. Through them and many other associates, I think that I have come to understand some of the joy and the sorrow, the difficulties and the possibilities of human community.

THE NEW COMMUNITY

I.

The Changing Scene

IN the middle of his recent book, *The Feast of Fools,* Harvey Cox devotes four or five pages to the subject of monastic communities.[1] Cox maintains that we are in need of a revival of the same spirit that gave birth to monasticism. His interest, of course, is not monasticism but the recovery of fantasy and festival in the whole society. The remarks about the monastic community are in the context of asserting that new forms of community must be developed for the survival of our world.

In most of what follows, the central topic will seem to be the religious order, but that is not my main interest. The subject of these essays is the Catholic church, its troubles and its possibilities. The religious order is my concern only insofar as it is an element embedded in a much larger problem. I intend to treat the religious order in relation to issues that far transcend it. My reason for speaking directly about the religious order is that it is the place where I stand and the terrain I know best. This perspective is a limited one, but the limitation guarantees that the perspective is a definite one. There are other issues that are as important or more important than those which I treat here, but they have to be dealt with from another point of view. A mother who has five children in the Catholic school could write a different book about the Catholic church, and we could

[1] See Harvey Cox, *The Feast of Fools* (Cambridge, 1969), pp. 88–93.

1

use more books of this kind. The present book is restricted to a style of life which is disproportionately represented by commentaries. Nonetheless, there still seems to be a deficiency of books that are proposing radical change in that way of life.

This work is written by someone in a religious order, and it will be read mostly by people in the same way of life. I would like to hope that it will reach a larger audience. Just as people in religious orders might profit by reading about the life of a mother of five, so people not in religious orders should be interested in what is happening to these orders. Although the details at time become intramural in concern, the main lines of this discussion should be of some significance to everyone interested in the church. It may be unfortunate, but it is fact nonetheless that the church's work, especially in fields like education, will largely be determined by what happens to religious orders.

The main issue before us, therefore, is no longer the reforming of the religious order but the refounding of the Catholic church. The statement is not intended to be sensationalistic; it is merely a statement establishing a context. The word refound is used to indicate a larger task than that suggested by words like renew, reform or adapt. There is no presumption here that a few people with messianic complexes are the ones to do the job. The church needs refounding in every age by all of its people. Continuity with the past is essential, and yet respect for the past not only allows but demands a re-examination of foundations. Those who love their tradition and believe in its future should be willing to criticize it at the deepest level and to work at its re-establishment for another age. "Only where chaos is overcome can what lies behind it emerge, and the seed of the fruit of chaos is perhaps more precious than the seed of any other fruit. Today there can be no hope for the future in any religion, art, or ethic that has not faced this threat of chaos."[2]

[2] Erich Neumann, *Art and the Creative Unconscious* (New York, 1966), p. 121.

2

Some people may think that the context of Catholic church is still too narrow a base of concern. It is true that the Catholic church can be a limitation upon one's outlook. It is also true here, however, that one must take a stand within some particular and concrete tradition. If one is a Catholic, one must take a stand where one is while working for a situation in which one's vision is broadened and not narrowed by Catholicism.[3] The Catholic church has a problem of living up to its name, that is, the claim to be catholic or universal. But it remains true that no realm of experience that is good for mankind is excluded in principle from Catholicism. Thus, working for a more open Catholic church can at the same time be a working for mankind. The important qualification is that the church must constantly be considered vis-à-vis the non-church world.

It is possible to drop out of all concern for the Catholic church. However, no sensitive person can entirely avoid the search for a new community with its overtones of a religious meaning. Where people go and how they face the era of new community is a personal choice that they must make for themselves. No judgments are implied on those who decide for something else. But this book directly refers to those who consider themselves Catholic and are associated with the religious order.

In writing previously on the religious order, my strongest conviction was the need not for a reshuffling of the design but for a leap from one level of design to another. I have borrowed a line of thought which Lewis Mumford, among others, has suggested to describe change in society as a whole. "The advance from the present constitution of society, with its confused mixture of the tribal, the civilized, the axial, the mechanistic, the national, will not be the outcome of any series of slight modifications or readjustments. Rather, the next transformation, it seems clear, will involve a leap from one plane to another. This will

[3] For a Catholic artist's reflections on this point, see Flannery O'Connor, *Mystery and Manners* (New York, 1969).

3

be similar to the decisive historic leap from the neolithic tribal community to a centralized state organization, focused in cities, capable of dominating and ordering a whole river valley. This emergence of a new system brings a change, not only in individual details, but in the over-all design."[4]

Half-hearted compromises and innumerable changes of detail are the enemy of everyone today. Whether people call themselves liberal, conservative or radical, it would seem that there could be agreement that some things are not working and are hurting the religious order. In this regard, people who are calling for change and those who oppose change are often much closer to agreement than they suppose. Both groups are opposed to an endogenous change, that is, a change on the same level that produces nothing essentially new and only upsets people. If there cannot be an exogenous kind of change that breaks through to a new level, then the future is perhaps better served by making fewer changes. Minor changes at the same level contribute to what Marcuse calls "repressive desublimation" which siphons off energy and domesticates the power to make significant changes. Whatever the future may hold, it certainly will not be reached by the frustration and pessimism springing from half-hearted compromise.

I have tried to put forward in these pages some suggestions for an exogenous kind of change. I make no claim that all change is good and that everyone must go along with whatever change is proposed. The assumption that change in social systems is both inevitably constant and necessarily good is of recent origin. The divinization of change is as narrow and short-sighted as an opposition to all change. However, the debate at this point in the church's history is not as to whether the system must inevitably change but how we are to direct the process of change that has already begun. The kind of proposal that

[4] Lewis Mumford, *The Transformations of Man* (New York, 1962), p. 143.

might be adequate to cope with this change is necessarily a threat as well as a promise. There is no guarantee beforehand that everything will work out all right. "The one thing that can be predicted of any true emergence is that its results cannot be predicted. In any emergent stage, the change in the basic pattern radically alters the nature of the constituent elements through their very shift in the position in the design, as well as by the fact that scattered mutations then become dominants, and forces that were once dominant become recessive or subordinate."[5]

What still characterizes the religious congregation in America is not a daring leap into the unpredictable but a plodding, prudent, whittling away of the life. One can sympathize with decision makers who are faced with the prospect of closing things. But simply to pull in one's resources is not a healthy way to live or even a hopeful way to die. One of the qualities which supposedly characterizes the religious order is mobility, that is, an ability to move quickly to a new project that needs doing. However, the image that the religious order projects today is one of a rigid and contracting system. The reason why the system is contracting is that it is assumed to be closed. A closed system here means that when a command is issued from the top, everything within the system adjusts accordingly. Actually, only the military, prisons, some hospitals, and a few other institutions can function that way in the contemporary world.[6] The religious order in the last few years has become an open system in which people do not adjust, gripe or rebel; they simply leave the system.

The religious order generally has a skeptical if not negative attitude toward the person who wishes to work differently or to live differently within the order. Evidence of his good intention has to be conclusively demonstrated. Today, however, it

[5] *Ibid.*
[6] See Erving Goffmann, *Asylums* (Garden City, 1961).

would be more sensible to make an assumption of good intention on the part of anyone trying to act differently, unless strong evidence to the contrary appears. Everyone else does not have to follow his lead but there should be breathing space for someone to work out his own personal style of life. The kind of person who has the initiative to work in new ways or to live in different fashion can usually stay with or leave the religious order equally as well. The presumption ought to be that if he is staying with the order it is out of loyalty and a sense of service.

This book is not an attack upon people who hold offices in religious orders; such personal attack would be unfair and fruitless. The book is in part an attack upon the concept of office in the orders. The distinction between a person and his office should not be difficult to make. It becomes a difficulty only when a person is a full time superior so that his identity comes to depend on the maintenance of the office. In such circumstances, it is practically impossible for anyone to advocate the elimination of his own job and when someone else advocates elimination of the job it is likely to appear as a personal attack. However, the elimination of the job or its complete overhaul may in the long run be healthier for everyone. People in positions of authority are generally struggling to do their best. What needs drastic change are the structural elements in the religious order. In this regard, the proliferation of committees and the multiplication of offices have not been very successful so far. No one should be very surprised. When an autocratic system spawns a committee structure under the haze of sharing power, the usual result is an increase of autocratic control. This is an instance of the domestication of a language (collegiality, subsidiarity, etc.) that effectively prevents the accomplishment of what the language demands. No power elite needs to enforce this control. Where there is insufficient imagination, technique and determination on the part of large numbers of people, the system conserves itself. A new way of thinking about "government" in religious orders is urgently needed. Unless the old system is turned upside down, the elaborate governments now being planned in religious orders will turn into monstrosities.

There is a difficulty in proposing large-scale change. One is never entirely sure of the audience that one is aiming for. Ideally, of course, one would like to speak to all of the people who are concerned with a problem. In fact, however, one can never do that. The people most likely to listen to a proposal for change and understand it may be the very people least able to bring about the change. Proposals at a theoretical level may very well add to the people's frustration. I have experienced this malaise with dozens of audiences on whom this kind of material has been tried. The reaction of an audience usually breaks neatly into two parts. One part of the audience nods agreement in the manner of saying: This kind of thing is so obvious that it hardly needs saying, but I am powerless to effect it. The other part of the audience indicates incomprehension; it is not so much a disapproval they show as an inability to make any connections between the words and their experience. Unfortunately, it is the latter group who still fill the great majority of positions of leadership.

Despite this difficulty, one must continue to suggest large-scale change. Social change must be large enough to shake the existing system but small enough to be in continuity with it. This is a precarious balance to maintain. Without vision the people die, but with vision and no hope the people are broken. Nevertheless, one must continue trying to support people's lives by speculation if that is one's job. One does so remembering Gabriel Marcel's statement that hope is real only where the possibility of despair exists. When the frightening, unasked questions are finally brought out into the open and candidly appraised, then hope has already become operative.

What is put forth in a book must in large part be theoretical

7

ideals. The phrase theoretical ideal does not necessarily refer to an elaborate abstraction which must be detailed in theory before being applied to life. Theoretical truth can be born out of concrete situations. "Practical application is a structuring element of truth itself" (H. G. Gadamer). When people say that they understand the theory but do not know how to apply it, one must ask whether there is not something wrong either with the theory or with the people's understanding of it. Sometimes, of course, a science can develop theory, all of whose practical ramifications are not immediately evident. The theory supplied in this book is not deduced from any science, although it does borrow from several sciences. For the main part, the truth that is sketched out here is elaborated from the way people are living. Instead of setting forth unreachable ideals, this book is to a great extent a do-it-yourself manual. At the least, some practical models are presented and some specific avenues of action are suggested.

Chapters II and III of this book set out data about the changing meaning of religion and of community. These two chapters do not deal expressly with the religious order but instead supply a background to which Chapters IV, V and VI can be related. These three chapters are addressed directly to the existing situation of religious orders. Specific changes are advocated that would move the religious order in the direction of the new religion and the new community. The seventh chapter attempts a synthesis and points toward a more radical program for the future.

If the context of discussion in the religious order were the church and mankind, then the questions asked would be considerably different from what they usually are. Right answers can hardly be gotten if the first questions asked are wrong ones. Even at very liberal groupings, the first question that is often asked is: What is a sister? If the question is legitimate at all, it can only be asked after a dozen questions of another kind have been raised. When people begin seriously to ask themselves: Who am I? Whom do I love? What do I want to do? How can we work together? then progress through questioning becomes possible. The desire to redefine what it means to be a sister is for the most part spurious. The definitions, however they are phrased, carry no weight of conviction. Worse still, they waste precious energy on an illusory project.

Sisters have been burdened with a stereotyped image that has provided them with an identity. It would be miraculous if any sister had fully escaped from the identity image that is still hammered home not only within the church but by the society at large. In trying to escape this identity many sisters begin looking for a new definition to offset the old one. The move is a logical but dangerous step. A new definition might be a slight improvement, but it would still be a "what" and not a "who." Sisterhoods still have far too much identity, and it is driving out the people who begin to ask who they are and whom do they love and what do they want to do. The premature asking about the identity of a sister will eliminate the very people who might demonstrate with their lives new ways of loving and working. Verbal definitions should be allowed to filter up in due time from newly established personal identity, group identity and organizational identity. The pertinent question of identity, Erikson writes, is: "What do I want to make of myself, and what do I have to work with?"[7]

I have singled out the sister in the above paragraphs not because the brother is exempt from the difficulty, but because the problem takes a considerably different form. Brothers do not have the sense of losing their identity because they never had much sense of one to begin with. At least, the larger society knew so little about their existence that it could not create a stereotype like that of the nun. Even the church has not paid much attention to the brother. The historical background is therefore very different for sisters and brothers, but the present premature seizing for a definition is the same. What

---

[7] Erik Erikson, *Identity: Youth and Crisis* (New York, 1968), p. 314.

had sustained brothers was a strong group solidarity. As the solidarity breaks down, no verbal definition will be a sufficient substitute.

If an organization of people is going to survive, it does have to develop a sense of social identity. A religious order in trying to do this probably has more life in its tradition and more power in its people than it gives itself credit for. If it were to build on that strength, it would have the time to re-establish a social identity. But it must trust in its own people to create this identity out of their lives. If people could stay with the order and ask "who am I," "whom do I love," and "what do I want to do," they might find interesting answers to those questions. The church in turn might be interestingly changed by such people. As things now stand, the person who asks these questions is usually edged out of the order, if not by intention nonetheless in fact. For example, a person cannot effectively ask "what do I want to do" unless he has a sufficient degree of control over the decision of where he is to work. Likewise, a person cannot ask "whom do I love" unless he can mix freely with members of both sexes.

The person who talks about the good or bad future of "religious life" usually presupposes that he knows quite clearly what he is talking about. I make no presumptions that anything is set beyond question. As I shall indicate in the next two chapters, people in religious orders must look forward to taking part in a new form of "religious life" that is emerging. Changing forms of sexuality, family life, social gathering, political party, work, leisure and education will all influence what comes to be in "religious life." A religious life of the future is one that will involve love personally and communally shared. It will also concern a work that is humanizing for the workers and helpful to the improvement of human conditions. Beyond these two elements one must be hesitant about including or excluding any particular structural elements.

10

One of the biggest obstacles to any change is an inability to break through categories that confine thinking within old patterns. Those people who seem to be in strongest rebellion against old stereotypes are often those who are most the victims of them. They have assimilated the old categories so well that the struggle is an internal one and the rebellion is contorted back against the rebel. Self-proclaimed radicals are often people who cannot think deeply enough to escape their own narrow and rebellious world. Some people who leave religious life do not leave at all, because now they are on the outside of *it* rather than the inside of *it,* but they are caught by *it* all the same. They could not figure out what a religious was and now they waste energy trying to find out what an ex-religious is. The way to get free of *it,* whether one stays or whether one leaves, is to redefine religious life not as an *it* at all but as people who can make of their lives what they will. Like everyone else, they start from where they are, and, like everything else, there are practical limits to how far their lives may change. Nevertheless, those limits can only be discovered by the people themselves. A person who is on his way to greater freedom may find that present boundaries of religious life are too oppressive to be tolerated. That person's leaving the religious order is probably a step of liberation. There are two other kinds of persons in religious orders today. On the one hand, there is the person who has no psychological space in which to move. He will suppose that the religious order is what confines him. He will be disappointed if he thinks that his freedom can be achieved simply by leaving the order. Departure from the religious order may be a helpful step, but at most it will be only one element in a quest for freedom. On the other hand, there is the person who already has the space in which to work through personal searching. If this person understands the religious order to be other people, then he may find as much freedom in staying as in leaving. At the same time, he may also have a greater field of service by staying with the people who have been the context of his life.

There is simply no framework into which people must be fitted. They have to discover their own sense of humanness and religiousness out of their own experience. Victor Frankl has written: "One should not search for an abstract meaning of life. Everyone has his own specific vocation or mission in life; everyone must carry out a concrete assignment that demands fulfillment."[8] It is no longer possible to have quasi-novitiates in which people would be fitted out with the proper attitudes and practices. Each person has to be given the greatest possible latitude to work out his own life style.

Many people think that the encouragement of unbounded individuality would mean the end of all communities and organizations. This conviction rests on the assumption that men ultimately are not communal and social beings. A main theme in the writings of Carl Rogers is that this assumption is quite false. "While the establishment of values by each individual may seem to suggest a complete anarchy of values, experience indicates that quite the opposite is true. Since all individuals have basically the same needs, including the need for acceptance by others, it appears that when each individual formulates his own values in terms of his own direct experience, it is not anarchy which results, but a high degree of commonality and a genuinely socialized system of values."[9] It is sometimes difficult to believe in this commonality, particularly when people are reacting against a false social conformity. There can be an interim period involving much conflict, alienation and idiosyncracy. During such a period, one needs more than a little trust in human nature and a strong belief that social unity can bear diversity and individuality.

Starting where people are does not necessarily mean accepting the traditional categories which they consider significant. I do

[8] Victor Frankl, *Man's Search for Meaning* (New York, 1963), p. 172.
[9] Carl Rogers, *Client-Centered Therapy* (Boston, 1951), p. 524.

not think that one must limit inquiry to the ideas that most people hold. Very often people's lives contain much more richness and possibility than do the conceptual patterns which they have been given. For many years an official language in religious orders limited the kinds of questions that could be asked. Many people knew that the language was inadequate because it left out most of the life people actually lived. Still, all the official things had to be said in the official language and none of the official words were allowed to die. Religious life needs desperately to let much of its language die.

Whatever be the feelings of most religious, I think that a discussion within the framework of the three vows is no longer viable. Any discussion that assumes that the vows constitute the one proper framework will not go very far. It is conceivable that one could redefine the word vow and the words poverty, chastity and obedience. One might manage to give to each word a positive and realistic meaning. Even if that could be done despite the burden of historical connotations, it is doubtful that the effort would be well placed. There would still be an effort here to separate out "religious life" from Christian life by a specific meaning given to poverty, chastity and obedience. In the past, a way of life that was thought to be particularly evangelical was described by the words poverty, chastity and obedience. Without rejecting the whole tradition, two things must be asserted for today: 1) all Christian life is a following of "evangelical counsels"; 2) no one's life is very well described by the words poverty, chastity and obedience.

One way of fighting to preserve something here has been to drop the first and third vows, keep the second and change its name from chastity to celibacy. I consider this move to be a disastrous rear guard activity. When it is said that *the* differentiating factor of the religious order is celibacy, it would appear that there is progress in understanding. At least we know what we are even if we do not particularly like what it is. But any discussion that begins with what we are is not going to go very far. Furthermore, the choice of the word celibacy as the *what* is destructive of further conversation. When all of the weight has been put on celibacy, then the seemingly simple task is to justify celibacy. All the energy is then wasted on the attempt to prove the value of this "state of life." It may be that all the members of religious orders will continue to be unmarried, but that is hardly the first thing to be said about who they are. Whether or not they do remain unmarried, the injection into the discussion of the word celibacy has been most unfortunate. There is no way to recover the meaning of a word that is burdened with negative connotations going back thousands of years.

The word celibacy had not regularly been used to describe the lives of sisters and brothers. It was picked up for them just when it was dying elsewhere. Of course, it is theoretically possible to apply the word to sisters and brothers, just as it is possible to apply spinster, bachelor, homosexual and other words. I suggest that none of these terms is appropriate or helpful. Each of them is burdened with certain inappropriate connotations.

Religious life had been described as one of vowed dedication to the service of God and neighbor. Despite the problems connected with the words poverty, chastity and obedience, these words supposedly designated qualities of Christian life. The religious order's claim was to live the gospel in a more direct and expressive way. The claim may have been arrogant but it was not narrow. The sudden stress upon the word celibacy has distorted the tradition. The choice not to marry may remain a *conditio sine qua non* for setting up adult communities of faith and dedication, or possibly there is room for a flexibility and diversity that has not been possible in past ages of the church. In any case, the word celibacy is not helpful to the discussion.

Any category which seems to close off some area of human experience must be approached skeptically. People eventually do settle for one part of life rather than another, but there is no reason why they should prematurely accept categories to define their life which exclude part of life. Christianity is supposed to be a choosing of all life by the way one chooses a particular life. The words that express this affirmation are faith, hope and charity. The evangelical life is a developing of these virtues which keep life open and developing further. Even these three virtues can become obstacles to life if they are treated as things to be acquired or demands to be submitted to. Generally, however, the words retain a good meaning and do not in principle exclude any segment of life. The concern of the following chapters is how people in religious orders might contribute to an increase of fidelity, trust and love. Whether at the end of such a contribution one will say that the religious order is finished or that it has been rejuvenated may be a debatable question. In either case, the most important job will have been done, namely, that each person will be able to contribute who he is to the growth of God's kingdom and each person will receive the affection and support he needs for life in God's creation.

There is today a general assumption that religious life was once relevant but is now no longer relevant. I think that quite possibly the opposite is true. What was done in the Middle Ages or post-Reformation age should have been done by the general Christian population. A two-storey spirituality was not helpful to anyone. The distinctiveness of the religious order lay in its community life, and that question had not been directly raised. As a result, its expressions were disfigured because the question was not clear and its contributions could not be accepted because the world was not ready. Only in the twentieth century have history and community arrived. The religious order, beset with the whole spectrum of human problems, finds itself all too painfully relevant to an age which hungers in affluence. The question for the religious community is not whether or not it is an anachronism but whether or not it has the intelligence and fortitude to be religious and to be a community.

15

II.

New Religion

SINCE most of what follows in this book is not theology, it may be helpful to set forth here the theological position that underlies the chapters to come. When people do not see language that is obviously religious, texts cited from holy scripture and exhortations to love God, they often assume that there is no theological perspective at work. One of the conclusions of this chapter will be that theology may be effective precisely when it is unobtrusively at work. Theology's role is not to inject some data which sociology or psychology has not had available, but it is to keep men aware that there may be more dimensions to their experience than what current fads assume. It must be sadly admitted, however, that theology has often, far from exercising this role, led the pack in hunting down the latest novelty. Yet theology somehow survives and comes back for another try at awakening the dreams of men. It is perilous to attempt a theological synthesis in a few pages, but several points about the current theological scene might be made here. I would hope that these points will make sense to someone who has been reading in theological literature and is trying to get a sense of the current direction of theology.

The struggle of Christian theology to get an adequate standpoint can be measured by its shifts in the use of the word religious. In *Experiences in Community* I pointed out the am-

16

biguity of this word and its consequent inappropriateness to describe the person in the religious orders of the Catholic church. I said there that the use of the word religious to describe these people says either too little or too much. Religious can be used in a perjorative sense to characterize a pre-rational and fear-ridden attachment to ritual, doctrine and law. In this sense of the word, people who are supposedly the avant-garde of the church should be the least religious of men. Obviously, there is another meaning of the word that is much more positive. The religious can refer to attitudes and expressions that sustain the human in its quest for some ultimacy in life. In this sense of the word, Christianity cannot look down upon the religious as less than itself nor fight religion as if it were an enemy. Instead, Christianity should ally itself with other belief structures in order to cultivate the religious. If this exalted meaning can be given to the word, it would seem pretentious for any group of people to call themselves the religious.

The ambiguity of the word religious is not simply the result of muddled thinking in theology. On the contrary, the preserving of the ambiguity may be part of theology's task. If there was a failure in recent theology, it was the attempt to corner the word religion so that Christianity could get a place to stand in directly opposing religion. This move was not only a case of theological overkill but a tactic with dangerous implications. It was supposed that the struggle in the world is between reactionary movements epitomized by religion and progressive secularizing forces led by technology. In such an alignment Christian theologians were keen on joining the latter team.

The argument for this description of opposing forces had some persuasiveness, but the limitations and dangers of this assumed arrangement should also have been obvious. What was finally being recognized was that Western technology was, if not a direct descendent, at least a step child of Christian attitudes in the West. Wholesale opposition within the church to science and technology had never been justified, and it was important to put an end to this error. On the other hand, an uncritical approval of technology today is not a proper stance either. There must be a similar balance when it comes to religion. It is valuable to know that religion outside the Judeo-Christian tradition has been largely characterized by a reactionary stand on social and political issues. However, we should also keep in mind that other religious traditions may have preserved contemplative attitudes and reverence for nature that were bulldozed in Western tradition.

The word religious has begun to regain much of its positive content. It is almost possible to use the word to refer both to an infra-Christian position and to a supra-Christian one. This use of the same word to characterize such divergent realities may seem like hopeless confusion. However, it seems to be a painful fact of human life that the ambiguity exists in language because it exists in life itself. There was a scholastic saying which pointed to a connection between the best and the worst in life. For example, the word power designates both a human and an inhuman reality. Power is a reality without which there is no life, and power is also a reality that destroys life. The most painful fact of all is that the two sides can never be entirely separated and the good side can become the bad with little realization on the part of the one using power. Similarly, religion can be expressive of what is best and most profound in human life but it can easily become inimical to life. One of the sure signs that this process is occurring is that the friends of religion are securely confident that they possess the best of things, instead of working humbly and continuously to make the ambiguous reality better.

Christian theology is at a stage of reconsidering its conclusion that the religious is bad and the secular is good. I would like to cite three external pressures upon theology that have encouraged this reconsideration. The three very divergent influences are: 1) sociology of religion, 2) ecology, 3) growing interest, especially among the young, in non-Western religion. These three things are not part of a single movement. In most respects they are unrelated to each other. At one place, however, they converge, and that is in challenging the assumption that progress is equivalent to more machinery.

Sociologists have generally been skeptical about the category of secularization as it has been used in recent theology. The word has seldom meant the same thing in theological and sociological writing.[1] Sociologists scoffed at the assumption in theology that religion was fast disappearing in our society. Furthermore, sociologists either could not understand or else refused to accept what Christian theology was saying about Christianity, namely, that it breaks out of the category of a religion. Theology was claiming that Christianity should not be lumped together with other systems of belief, ritual and practice; that belief, ritual and practice in Christianity have a function almost the opposite of what they have in other religions.

I think that theology had a point here which sociology continues to neglect. Nevertheless, sociology has exercised a corrective role in theology's first narrowing the word religion and then pronouncing it both dying and worthy of death. Theologians may like to say that Christianity is not "merely one of the religions," but sociology has a stronger position in saying that in fact it has been just that. Sociologically, Christianity has borne more similarities to than differences from other religions. However, this fact is not necessarily so bad as much of recent theology has claimed. Theologians should perhaps be a little more cautious about pressing the claim that Christianity contradicts other religions. They should first listen to the sociology of religion and the history of religion to appreciate some of the strong points and the good functions of religion.

The second influence upon theology's reconsideration of the

[1] See David Martin, "Toward Eliminating the Concept of Secularization," in *Penguin Survey of the Social Sciences 1965,* ed. by J. Gould (Baltimore, 1965), pp. 169–82.

religious has been from the unexpected sphere of ecology, that is, the study of an organism's interaction with its environment. Religion has always been tied in to the cycle of nature and the preservation of cosmic harmony. Technology thus appeared on stage as an enemy of religion. In this confrontation recent theology has tended to side with technology. It would still seem to be valid that technology should be considered more a friend than a foe of Christian faith, but the way that technology has developed to the detriment of human community casts doubt upon the intimacy their relationship should have. Technology can be of service only when it is clearly subservient to a greater human context, but there is a growing suspicion that in technology man has created a frankenstein that is out of control. At such a point of history, the role of Christianity should have been an intelligently critical one rather than a belatedly encouraging one. In Theodore Roszak's blanket attack upon our technological culture, he lays the blame partly upon Christianity: "The trouble is, we don't trust to the way of the world. We have learned— in part from the accelerating urbanization of the race, in part from the objective mode of consciousness so insistently promulgated by Western science, in part, too, perhaps from the general Christian disparagement of nature—to think of the earth as a pit of snares and sorrows. Nature is that which must be taken unsentimentally in hand and made livable by feverish effort, ideally by replacing more and more of it with man-made substitutes."[2]

I suspect that Roszak's reference here is to the earlier puritanical attitude of the churches toward human nature. His attack would be even more appropriate against recent theological writing which tried to exalt man at the expense of nature. In a paradoxical aspect of theology's glorying in "the worldly" it has implicitly left the sub-human world exposed to control,

[2] Theodore Roszak, *The Making of a Counter-Culture* (New York, 1969), pp. 249f.

domination and exploitation by man. In stressing man's freedom to create a new world it has appealed to certain instincts in Western man that were already over-cultivated; that is, the tendency to do violence to the environment in the name of a mechanical and economic progress.

The bill for centuries of exploiting the land is beginning to come home in America. Nearly all of us live oblivious to what is catching up with us, but time is running out and there is no place left for us to run. The violence done to the air and the water and the land will not disappear as one more passing fad of concern. The results continue to accumulate daily and there is a limit which will certainly be reached unless a massive change of attitude occurs first. In this situation, theology has to ask itself whether it has been on the right side in recent conflicts over progress. The American Indian believed in the great earth spirit which should be reverenced. The Indian may not have had the full truth but he may have had an important truth that the new settler had overlooked.

Israel arose in struggle against nature-worshipping tribes and the gods of space, nature and myth. Judaism, as Christianity after it, was an urban phenomenon. It appealed to the people who were separating themselves from the land.[3] The God of Israel was the Lord of history, a god clearly distinct from the agricultural techniques of the Canaanites and the sacred shrines on the mountains. But this Lord is not the god of the city as opposed to the country, not the god of time instead of space, not the god of machines over nature. He is the Lord of all who breaks man's bonds with nature so that man can then love nature as his origin and continuing source of life. Man cannot go back to nature but neither can he leave it; he must reverence it in the act of transforming it. Lewis Mumford writes: "Now that man understands these primordial connections, he must

[3] See Max Weber, *On Charisma and Institutional Building* (Chicago, 1968), pp. 240f.

acknowledge his old debt to his partners throughout the whole range of organic creation, his constant dependence upon their activities, and not least his link with his own original nature. Though he is now the dominant species, his fate is still bound up with the prosperity of all forms of life; and he carries his own animal organs and his natural history into every ideal future that he projects. They, too, partake of the divine impetus and approach the divine goal."[4]

The third pressure upon theology is in some ways allied to the previous one. Partly through the small but growing tide of anti-technology and partly through world-wide communication (made possible by technology), there is a new interest in the religious teaching and practice of the non-Western world. Courses in oriental religion, history of religions, and comparative religion have a growing popularity in universities. There is interest at a very practical level in the mystical and contemplative states that are part of the heritage of the East. The use of drugs is intimately connected to this movement, and the drug experience is nearly always described in mystical and religious terms. This phenomenon can no longer be dismissed as pertaining to a handful of extreme cases. *The New York Times* recently carried a headline which asked: Is opium the religion of the people?

At a time when Christian theology was frantically trying to get itself "relevant" to the age, many of the younger generation were deciding that the age was not worth being relevant to. The thing to do with the present scene, they concluded, was not to be relevant to it but to change it. They set out to change the situation by refusing to accept the tools which the situation presented. They chose instead to be dramatically and abrasively irrelevant to what are supposedly the major concerns of American life. How much naïveté and delusion there is in this counterforce is not my concern here. What is certain is that a

4 Mumford, *op. cit.*, p. 24.

new interest in religious attitude, ritual and symbol has crept in from a most unlikely quarter. This development has not meant much of a gain for the established Protestant and Catholic churches. More often than not, they are seen as part of the enemy establishment.

It might almost be said that the Bonhoeffer opposition of Christianity to religion has come full circle. In the thinking of some young people, Christianity is indeed allied with the secular as the enemy of religion, but it is now the latter and not the former where hope for man resides. The church again becomes the infamy, but this time not because she is unreasonable but because she is too reasonable, not because she has too much faith but too little of it, not because she does not fit into the world but because she fits into it all too neatly. It is probably true that just as the previous stage of opposing religion was a case of overkill, so a new stage that is anti-church is also exaggerated. There is undoubtedly much to learn from non-Christian tradition, but it is just as certain that there is much to be learned from the history of Christianity. The Christian churches may have done badly in their history but their mistakes were human mistakes and they had better be appreciated as such by those who would build a better world.

In summary, Christian theology is now developing a new sensitivity to the meaning of religion. The task is not to return to "primitive religion" but to reconsider whether all such religion can be dismissed as primitive. Religion, I have suggested, is something that may function at an infra-rational, pre-scientific stage but it is also something that may function at a supra-rational, post-scientific stage. Of course, the latter will appear to be no more relevant to our age than the former. Nevertheless, what is most genuinely and ultimately relevant to an age is seldom recognized by those who talk endlessly of relevance. Christianity, if it has any trust in its own mission, ought to align itself with those forces which oppose the arrogance of a culture that devastates the earth in the name of progress. Positively, it ought to join hands with the social and political movements that try to create a context where the maximum of human potentiality can be unlocked.

Theology in the last part of the twentieth century will have the job of trying to keep a full perspective on man and the world. This full perspective has not functioned in the past because it was not yet available. It is to be hoped that the kind of influences cited above will keep theology from its flirtations with one-sided answers. Theology is always a groping in the dark toward a door one hopes is there. Finding a comfortable chair to sit down in is a relief but also a danger. The very confidence with which new developments are pounced upon in theology is indicative of a distortion of perspective.

There is general agreement that in the late nineteenth century there was a liberalizing trend in most Protestant and much Catholic theology. Differences with others were played down, the philosophy of the age took over and doctrine took second place. The twentieth century witnessed a strong orthodox reaction that stressed the specificity of Christian faith, the uniqueness of Jesus and the need for divine mercy. But neo-orthodoxy in Protestantism has passed and a new era in Catholicism was opened with Vatican II. Now a bewildering variety of theological positions present themselves. Nearly all of them try to be both "post-liberal" and "post-orthodox," but that is more easily proposed than disposed. The demands of journalistic style and the TV camera have not been helpful to the development of a carefully elaborated and well-nuanced theology.

A few months after *The New York Times* had heralded the death of God theology, it announced on its front page that the "theology of hope" was now replacing the "death of God." The implication that theology moves in a sequence of schools was misleading, although the rash of paperbacks on any such "school" lends credence to the belief that theology does move in this way. A phrase such as "death of God" may mean something profound in the writing of Nietzsche, Hegel and Luther. A few people in the 1960's may have spoken profoundly of the "death of God" before the words became a cant phrase. To describe a theological school with the words is practically a *reductio ad absurdum.* In a similar development, an attention to hope as an element of Christian theology was overdue. But the suggestion that theology has after all these years found its proper object in hope is not well founded. The implicit claim that theology must center on hope or else be utterly outdated is pretentious. Theology should among other things be hopeful, but theology is about God and everything related to God. There are many more ways to approach the subject than that taken by a few experts on hope.

No alternative school or movement is advocated in this essay. The theology that will continue to be the most effective will be a theology that is drawing upon the best of past tradition. It is also a theology that speaks from a critical standpoint today, sensitive to the widest possible set of experiences. Langdon Gilkey writes: "Meaningful symbols must be symbols of life, and so a meaningful system of theological symbols must continually be related beyond its own formal range to the stuff of life to which they bring illumination. What is said about God on the basis of faith must be related to what is felt and experienced by man in the ordinary stuff of his life—and that means a theological method far wider than that provided by the older Word of God or the newer hermeneutical theologies of the continent of Europe."[5]

What I would like to suggest at this point is that Christian theology must not lose touch with a few profound experiences of human life. In being profound they are also ambiguous. As described in the first part of this essay, these are the ambiguities

[5] Langdon Gilkey, *Naming the Whirlwind: The Renewal of God-Language* (New York, 1969), p. 201.

25

which theology tried to short-circuit out of itself. A Christian theology that will be more adequate than the past theologies will have to maintain a tension between different aspects inherent to human life. It is easy to preach a religion of joy, and it is also possible to spread a religion of sorrow, but Christian theology ought to deal with an experience that fuses joy and sorrow into one. It was once possible to have a religion of weakness, and it was recently fashionable to have a religion of strength, but Christianity ought to be neither of those because it is the union of both. Of course, this combination of opposites does not seem logical at all. As a result, any systematically developed ideology fails at some point when it is measured against life as a whole. "Life seems in a baffling and mysterious way to share both creativity and sin, wonder and terror, joy and despair—and in the midst of its fateful tragedy to reveal facets of hope, renewal and love. This strange characteristic of life, secularism seems not to comprehend—with its alternating optimism about man's rational and moral powers as a maker of history, and its despair at our loneliness in a cold, ruthless world. We are neither so good and so powerful as the optimistic secularist says, nor is life so empty and futile as the pessimistic secularist declares."[6]

The experience of the Jewish prophets culminating in the experience of Jesus of Nazareth was that life lived in the highest intensity did not negate the divine but affirmed it. It is neither strength nor weakness that leads to God but an experience of weakness that is recognized as man's ultimate strength and a kind of strength that chooses weakness or dependence upon others. In reaction to a "god of the gaps" who attacks man in his weakness and fills up his need, there has been much talk about a god who meets man in his strength. But man strong and confident is just as much a distortion as man weak and anxious. The true man is revealed only when one experiences

[6] *Ibid.*, p. 259.

simultaneously weakness and strength: then one can meet a god who is so powerful that he can be powerless. Both strength and weakness can lead away from God when one is separated from the other; both strength and weakness can be the way to God when one is of a kind that leads to the other.

The tension between opposite sides of experience is perhaps best demonstrated in the life of the prophet Jeremiah. "We encounter him in the pit of utter agony and at the height of extreme joy, carried away by divine wrath and aching with supreme compassion. There are words of railing accusation and denunciation; the lips that pleaded for mercy utter petitions for retribution, for the destruction of those who stand in the way of the people accepting his prophetic word. Indeed, the commission he received at the time of his call endowed him with the power to carry out two opposite roles: 'To pluck up and to break down, to destroy and to overthrow, to build and to plant' (1:10)."[7] It was not a case of moodiness that led the prophet to say at one moment: "My heart is broken within me, and my bones are out of joint" (23:9), and at another moment: "Thy words became a joy to me, the delight of my heart" (15:16). It is rather the experience of a living fire within him that overflows with joy and weariness (20:9). The joy and the sorrow are not separate acts; they are dual aspects of a single experience of life at its most profound.

It is most of all in love that man experiences at once the ecstasy of life and the agony of death. Freud rediscovered the mythological connection between love and death.[8] In love there is an experience of mortality and yet a hoping against hope that love is stronger than death. Here no science of man gives answers; out of the experience originates man's mythology and religion. The ambiguity of religion emerges again, either as a pre-rational, fear-ridden escape or as a post-rational and courage-

[7] Abraham Heschel, *The Prophets* (New York, 1969), vol. I, p. 125.
[8] See Rollo May, *Love and Will* (New York, 1969), pp. 99–121.

ous gift of self. Some men believe in a reality beyond their life because they have no love of life; other men believe in a beyond because they love life so much. Men who have no love and care of this world prefer to retreat into another world where all problems are absent. But there can also be a belief in a beyond death because love is experienced as stronger than death. Such a belief leads not to escape from this world but to deeper immersion in it. One who believes in life struggles every moment against death in order that life should finally triumph over death. He does not escape from the reality of death by first escaping from the reality of life. He finds it difficult to believe in any life beyond death, but he finds it more difficult to believe that death is final conqueror of all. If Christian theology were in touch with this kind of experience it would not panic when confronted with the claim: Belief in an afterlife is a myth which cannot be believed by twentieth-century man. Undoubtedly there are men today who cannot believe in this myth, but their deficiency should not be made the norm of human experience.

The simple human experience described above ought to be the center of theology. It is not a promise which is central to theology but the experience of life which is both threat and promise. Life is hoping and despairing, beautiful and ugly, free and determined, dying and going beyond death. A world without God keeps ripping away one side or the other and veers wildly from optimism to pessimism and back again. A theology that claims to believe in a personal, creative force should be able to maintain both sides at once. It has often failed at this task. For example, in emphasizing the personal, free and historical character of Christianity, it tended to exclude the impersonal, determined and mythical elements of human experience. The correction, of course, is not to go back to the mythical or the impersonal, but to achieve a new synthesis of the free and the determined, nature and history, the personal and impersonal.

Creating such a synthesis is the great problem in theology.

Anything that is presented as the all embracing framework is proved to be too narrow by the very fact that it can be set out in words and concepts. It is only by working from several directions and with a variety of images that one can hope to reach a point that is relatively comprehensive and always open to further elaboration. I suggest that two words which are central to theology and must be rediscovered again are person and presence. Both words have suffered from their vague use in clichés; both are assumed to have been exhausted by premature definitions. The words are literally inexhaustible in meaning and the meaning has hardly been touched.

Person has been a major theme in twentieth-century thought. Unfortunately, it often seems to be assumed that person is one category of one school of philosophy. Furthermore, the way "personalism" has developed, it usually seems to be asocial if not anti-social. It speaks much of the personal and interpersonal but these remain unrelated to the natural, social and institutional framework in which men live. In order to establish the personal at all there has to be a clear break with nature; man is not just a "sport" in a world of things. But if it is true that nature flows into man and man is nature's epitome and guide, then man must discover all the relationships that structure his life. Beyond the stage of nature and the stage of individualized man is the plane of a humanized cosmos or a cosmicized man. This will truly be a new stage of things that has never been experienced before. A kind of bio-politics becomes the key to the person and the person for the first time becomes the key to the universe. What the Greeks could dimly foresee in making man the measure of all things can now be filled in by a developed anthropology on a world-wide scale. Truth becomes biographical, but instead of this leading to an arbitrary subjectivism, each man's biography interlocks with the whole universe.

The mode of being for person is presence and the mode of being for cosmicized man is a new richness of presence. The word presence has often functioned in a vague and murky way. When the present was spoken of, it was assumed to be a point on the time sequence. But presence is the mode of being for persons. Present refers to time and it refers to space, but it also refers to a way of being related to others. It is this last way that is primary and subsumes the other two. Because a man is present to others he has a temporal present. This presence in time refers to the way he relates the past and the future. We now have a greater presence possible because of all that we know about the facts of the past and the possibilities of the future. A denigration of the present in favor of the future implies a misunderstanding of both. Man's choices are to accept the present as best he can or to try to reject the present. To the extent that he accepts his present he discovers the full range of bodiliness, his relation to space and time and his relation to all men.

Christian theology must look for its adequate object of study not in a text or in an object but in the person with all of his presence. God speaks man, a language which man does not fully understand. In studying the person as he is most present, man will find the texts and the objects, the past and the future, death and resurrection. The discovering of that present, personal life will reveal how the ambiguities of joy and sorrow, weakness and strength, life and death, can be held together. The man who is present to life, Hugo Rahner has written, "is a man with an easy gaiety of spirit, one might also say a man of spiritual elegance, but he is also a man of tragedy, a man of laughter and tears, a man indeed of gentle irony, for he sees through the tragically ridiculous masks of the games of life and has taken the measure of the cramping boundaries of our earthly existence."[9]

It is probably evident from the preceding that if religion refers to this kind of experience available in all lives, then Christianity is at best only one means of interpreting this experience. Much of Christian theology, even when it claims to

[9] Hugo Rahner, *Man At Play* (New York, 1967), p. 27.

be avant-garde, is an elaboration of a doctrine which dictates to life. Christian theology must now enter a new era of ecumenism which will be far broader in its implications than anything imagined when Catholics and Protestants began their first conversations. The dialogue will be between the Christian past and the total environment of the personal present. The truth which is affirmed in this religion must be biographical in its concreteness and universal in its scope.

Christian theology thus has the task of looking for the divine in history, but not in one strip of history or by one version of history. The history to be used will no longer be the British or American version; it will finally be a human history. This history as the encounter of all peoples is something quite new. It can even be quite humiliating to those who have perched above history and interpreted everything from their fixed point of dominance.[10] History is in a sense only now beginning. Everything up to now has been tribal reporting because the record of the human race has not been available. Henceforth, Christianity, instead of talking much about the history in which God reveals himself, will have to test its faith by living in human history. A genuine conversation with all religious traditions will soon be feasible.

Christian theology is not very well prepared for this meeting, although it is rapidly learning. It is beginning to realize that there can be a mythical and symbolic kind of history which is at least as true as our highly rational version. It is beginning to learn about an appreciation of nature and the value of wonder. But it has yet to relinquish its solid footing outside human history where it exercises final judgment upon everything. It still measures life against some doctrine instead of the other way around.

Roman Catholicism, in particular, has hardly begun to face

[10] See Mircea Eliade, *The Quest: History and Meaning in Religion* (Chicago, 1969), p. 51; "Cultural Fashions and the History of Religion," in *History of Religions* (Chicago, 1967), pp. 21–38.

up to the historical limitation of all of its doctrine. This fact has seldom been clear in arguments over this or that papal statement. Even liberal theologians have avoided the issue by talking about infallible and "non-infallible" pronouncements, instead of attacking head on the assumptions which underlie any pronouncements of truth. The Catholic church has reluctantly admitted that the scriptures are not a set of divinely revealed truth but are instead a highly inspired literature. That the statements of councils are not pronouncements of God would seem even more obvious, but this fact is difficult to admit since they are such poor literature as well. When the church is ready to let go of these securities and face up to her human position, then she may discover what it means to be a "holy people" by dialogue with other people. This would not be a rejection of her tradition but rather a drawing upon the tradition that still lives in the people of the church.

Christianity should at least be engaged in serious talk with Judaism, if only to understand Christianity's own foundations. Jewish thought and writing still seem to exercise very little corrective upon the arrogant assumption by the church that the Hebrew scriptures are a Christian book. All of the recent "old testament" study by Christians has not undone the biases which run very deep in Christianity. In fact it may have strengthened the conviction that the Jews were an ancient people who prepared the way for Christ. It is thought that if they did not have enough sense to accept their messiah, they ought at least to have had the graciousness to disappear after Christ. From the first moment of Christianity's existence it has been able to define itself by opposing Judaism. There is a certain value in this for achieving one's self-identity, but in the long run that kind of self-identity is not worth having.

Christian theology might have saved itself some trouble if it had heeded the warnings of Jewish theologians against an intoxication with the secular.[11] Judaism had already been over that route centuries ago, having been driven there by Christian pressures. Christianity might have preserved a sense of reverence for nature, law and religious experience if it had kept in touch with Judaism. Christianity is still a long way from recovering what it means to be a holy people. In contrast, throughout all of Judaism's incredible sufferings it has kept alive the mysterious lordship of Yahweh and the searing message of the prophets. The continental theology that still dominates American circles has little living contact with Jewish life and thought. Both because of the concentration of Jews in parts of America and the peculiar history of American Christianity, the dialogue between Jew and Christian can hardly take place except in America.[12]

The wider ecumenism will mean a conversation with those who belong to non-Western religions and those who reject affiliation with any religious institution. As I have described earlier, there is clearly a religious movement outside the churches and in large part opposed to the churches. This movement is not without its illusions but it is also not without a truth that the churches have yet to learn. The churches have set boundaries that are too narrow and enforced those limits in an external way.

The change needed in the church is in one sense very simple. It must become a community of belief with all of the offices administered by and through the community. This is a more difficult project than one would first suppose because there is a great amount of fear and vested interest which opposes any move in this direction. Nevertheless, Christianity has survived through the centuries, and today the teaching and example of

[11] See Emil Fackenheim, "A Jew Looks at Christianity and Secularist Liberalism," in *The Restless Church,* ed. by W. Kilbourn (Philadelphia, 1966), pp. 86–99.

[12] See Herbert Richardson, *Toward An American Theology* (New York, 1967), pp. 108–132.

Christ, the faith and the hope he engendered, are more alive than ever. It remains to be seen whether his followers can situate these ideals in the full range of human history. "Christianity is not a religion which brings 'God' into the equation of human existence, using him as a known integer as one totals up the results. It is rather a religion which sets man face to face with the Incomprehensible which pervades and encompasses his existence and makes it impossible for him to construct an ideology —concerning the ultimate nature of religion—wherein he maintains that there is a calculable root formula of existence which man himself can manipulate and out of which he can build existence."[13]

Life is just as mysterious as in the past and no closer to solution by any calculation. The experience of love and hate, joy and sorrow, hope and despair, dying and rising still demand that there be more to life. Christianity ought to set men free for that quest, giving them the courage to believe that it is not senseless to seek and to build. Christian theology is going to play a humbler role than it has been accustomed to; it will be a resource for those who find its interpretations helpful. Christianity as a whole will function in a lesser role but perhaps one truer to its nature. It must try to understand human life out of its own lights and in cooperation with all men who sense the worth of a humanized world.

[13] Karl Rahner, *Belief Today* (New York, 1967), p. 111.

III.

New Community

THERE are not many words used as frequently today as the word community. It is a word used with some degree of scientific precision in sociology. It is also a term tossed about with casual abandonment in international affairs. Community sometimes seems to be put forward as the answer to all problems of the disaffected youth in the nation. Most strikingly at present, community has become a rallying cry of educational reform. Out of this last use emerges the connection of the word with the struggle for minority rights to the extent that in some places "the community" designates a racial unit.

The difficulty under which this book and especially this chapter labors is this extraordinary ambiguity of the word community. The fact that the word spans a wide range of meaning may indicate the rich human phenomenon that is at stake. All of the best, simple, human words are rich precisely in being ambiguous. With respect to the word community, however, one suspects that, instead of it evoking rich connotations, it has become a cant phrase bearing no particular meaning. My difficult task in this chapter is to try to assign some definite meaning to the word community. There is a touch of arbitrariness to the choice of a meaning but it is not a whimsical choice that I make. The value of the meaning given to the word will be determined by the consistency with which it can be used and the range of data with which it can be helpful.

35

Although some of the literature referred to in this chapter is sociological in nature, this is not a sociological essay on community. The word is most often used in sociology to refer to a town or a section of a city. Consequently, units that are smaller than this are usually called sub-communities. For reasons which should become clear I use the word in a related but different sense. I am trying to suggest by my usage that the sociological changes reflect a deeper philosophical change in thinking about community. Besides sociological issues, therefore, there are psychological and philosophical questions that are unavoidable when one investigates the com-union of men. In talking about a philosophical ideal of community, I shall also refer to the contribution which Christianity has made to the emergence and preservation of this (mostly unrealized) ideal. The hope for mankind that has haunted much philosophy of a "community of communities" has been buttressed by Christianity when it has functioned at its best.

In this chapter I am interested in that ideal of community which is not new but is being newly attended to. Correlative with this newly recognized ideal are some novel attempts to embody the ideal. The conscious connection between the ideal of community and the experiments in community is the phenomenon of "new community." I shall first advert to the recent history which has brought us to the contemporary scene. Second, I shall attempt a descriptive definition of the new community. Third, I shall discuss some characteristics of this community.

The issue of community on the contemporary scene is so all pervasive that it is difficult to single out individual examples of the problem. At those spots where the word community emerges and where people talk somewhat obsessively of "building community," there is revealed only the most obvious case of what is present nearly everywhere. In fact, it is very likely that the most intense struggles for community take place without the word intruding at all.

If one wishes to have examples of the struggle for community, the contemporary cinema offers them in abundance. While the grand Hollywood spectacles have been failing at the box office, a series of low cost films from small firms have been extraordinarily successful. What nearly always characterizes the latter kind of film is the study of a microcosmic quest of man for community.

One movie that is especially pertinent here because it is so self-conscious is *Alice's Restaurant.* The film is a semi-documentary about a group of people who try to live together in—of all places—a church. When things have gone wrong, they plan a great celebration at which Alice and her husband Ray are married again. But something is still wrong at the end of the picture as the young people depart. At this point Alice's husband makes the most telling comment. He says that he wishes he could get a large tract of land in Vermont; everyone would then be able to live as one happy family and not get on one another's nerves. This is one of the oldest of romantic beliefs that wide open spaces would solve our human problems. What makes the film's remark ludicrous is that the hope in open space is not voiced in Harlem, New York but in Stockbridge, Massachusetts. Changing the location of one's problems from Stockbridge to Rutland is hardly a radical enough solution to age-old human difficulties.

The connection of community with space and place is an ancient one. Particularly in America, people have a strong sense of space.[1] A community is understood to be a place in which one lives. When a community has problems, the way to deal with them is to move further out into the country. America from its birth has been a space conqueror, whether the space was the western frontier, outer suburbia, or the Sea of Tranquility. The keen sense of space has unfortunately been accompanied by a weak sense of time. This imbalance poses a problem

[1] See Sydney Mead, *The Lively Experiment: The Shaping of Christianity in America* (New York, 1963).

37

as the empty space diminishes. Perhaps many Americans can still feel an expansiveness to life by looking at the earth from the viewpoint of the moon. But there are millions of Americans crowded into urban ghettos who have no sense of physical and psychological space in which to develop a community. This crowding of people and the consequent explosiveness of the urban situation is a new phenomenon in America. The founding fathers had great hopes for America because they were convinced that men here would be both virtuous and wealthy. The Calvinist settlers believed that because America was God's new chosen people they would be blessed with the abundance of the land. The Deists believed that because men were blessed with the wealth from the land they would be virtuous. In either case, the new man in America was to be both good and rich. The messianic sense of being God's chosen people subduing the land has not died easily.[2]

The close relation of a community to a place has a high degree of realism to it. A people is formed in large part by its geography. The land provides the sustenance for human community and the stability to orient human life. Men sink their roots into a place and it gradually acquires the sacredness of its domestication and tradition. The land becomes for its inhabitants not a place but *patria, heimat,* or *home.* To "fight for one's country" has been a badge of honor in the past. Men have gone to every extremity when it was a matter of protecting their homeland.

In many of the large, old cities of America it still seems to make sense to speak of communities located in a certain place. For example, in New York, the West Village, the Upper East Side, Harlem, East New York, or Highbridge are not just sections of a city. The names designate styles of life and different

<hr>

[2] See Reinhold Niebuhr, *The Irony of American History* (New York, 1962); Dorothy Dohen, *Nationalism and American Catholicism* (New York, 1967).

ways of being human. They sometimes seem to be different civilizations except that there remain some political, economic and social ties which throw them into a precarious kind of unity. Thus, it would be too easy to say that New York City is not a community but Harlem is. It is not clear that Harlem itself is a unit or that 125th Street is a community. Even those who are genuinely interested in working with local communities have difficulty in determining where is the community and who speaks for it.

The thing that should be evident in this discussion is that community does not simply mean a piece of land so that everyone living on that land is part of the community. There is a challenge everywhere in the world today to the assumption that place determines community. In this regard it is interesting to view the parochial problems of the Christian church. The word church is supposed to be a name for a community, that is, the people called together in Christ. More popularly, however, the word church refers to a building. The parish is called the local community and it is supposedly composed of the people who live on that segment of land. The "church universal" is not supposed to be divided into parts; instead, the universal is to be embodied in miniature in each of the little church communities. The little churches, however, have arisen on a territorial basis and the territories may not make much sense as population shifts.

It is no secret that the local church is in trouble but there is little admission of how deep the problem runs. The difficulties which the church is experiencing spring from the very way the church is divided. Place as *the* determining factor for community no longer holds true. Although place is an important factor, it is still only one factor in the question of community. My point refers not only to the urban dweller with his high mobility. In fact, the central city may have more cause for maintaining local churches that bring together people who might otherwise not meet. Nevertheless, for city dweller, suburbanite and rural American, a different way of relating to his place has sprung up and the churches have not been very sensitive to the change.

I have already indicated the main theme which runs throughout this chapter. There has been a dramatic shift in this century which has come from the distinction between man and his place. In Robert Park's study of Chicago early in this century, he distinguished three aspects or levels of community, namely, the biotic (functional and work aspects), the moral (kin and social ties), and the spatial (tie of land and neighbors).[3] Park pointed out that in earlier stages of history these three aspects of community had overlapped but that in modern Chicago they tended to separate. It is a little misleading to say that they had overlapped because the distinction between those aspects had hardly been made at all before this century. The three may have co-existed but it was the spatial that had taken primacy.

So complete was the identification of community and place that the question of community was thematized for inquiry only when men and their turf began to separate in dramatic fashion. Toward the end of the nineteenth century, the well-known distinction between "community" and "society" was elaborated. By this distinction philosophers and sociologists were pointing out that there are two main ways for the individual person to relate to a group of people. It is evident that the word community had some moral overtones to it and designated the more human and humanizing type of association. "Relationships within community have been described as 'organic' and 'natural' while societal relationships are seen as 'mechanical' and 'rational.' . . . Thus did Tonnies distinguish between *Gemeinschaft* (community) and *Gesellschaft* (society), the former based on shared intimacy and interdependence—the folkways and mores

---

[3] For a summary of this study, see Maurice Stein, *The Eclipse of Community* (New York, 1960), pp. 13–46.

of primary groups; the latter signifying impersonal, logical, formally contractual relationships inherent in commerce, science and bureaucracy. Tonnies helps to clarify the distinction by asserting that in community human relationships are characterized by acquaintance, sympathy, confidence and interdependence, whereas in society relationships reveal strangeness, antipathy, mistrust and independence."[4] I think that the stark opposition between these two realities needs challenging, but the distinction itself represented progress in understanding. The distinction between society and community provided a framework of discourse for considering the elements of community.

The main model which was presumed at the time this distinction was made was the village or small town. In the village was available a simple network of human relationships. This world was one in which people met face to face, knew each other's business, and felt that they belonged to the place. What rightly worried thinkers of the time was that the human order of communities was in a process of disintegration. Men were being uprooted from the land and torn from the organism of kin and neighbors. Industrialization, urbanization, and bureaucratization were moments of the same process and all of them spelled the end of small town life. Thinkers at the turn of the twentieth century caught a glimpse of what was to come. Almost without exception they looked forward bleakly to a time when, in the McLuhanesque phrase, there would be no place to go home to. "Sociologists like Weber and Tonnies were too realistic to think the change could be stopped, but neither could they hide their nostalgia for a past where, if there was less affluence, there was more humanity, and if there was more social control, there was also more social support."[5]

Today we have reached the stage at which the whole country

[4] Fred Newmann and Donald Oliver, "Education and Community," in *Religion and Public Education* (Boston, 1967), p. 186.

[5] Andrew Greeley, *The Crucible of Change* (New York, 1968), p. 73.

is urbanized. This statement may seem to be an exaggeration, particularly if one is familiar with northern New England or the great Southwest. However, the statement refers not to a claim that everyone lives in cities but to the fact that the quality of life which characterizes the city is inevitably spreading throughout the whole country. Urbanization refers first of all to the fact that the country is controlled from giant centers of economics, politics, communication and education. Only in isolated spots is there a small-town America, and it is doomed. Those who hate the city may bewail the passing of small-town America. They are not without cause for their dismay. The march of the city has swallowed up much that was good in the village. But the values of another age that are worth preserving cannot be saved by constructing romantic anachronisms. In this context, the suburban area that tries to carry on as if it were a small town would be funny if it were not tragic.

There is no intention here of attacking people who live in suburbia. Most people are there simply because this is the best option they have among limited alternatives. But something has gone drastically wrong when a man has to spend a very large part of his life traveling to and from his work. The supposed values of the "suburban community" are lost as suburbia moves further out beyond the decaying urban sprawl. Life gets built around the excrescences of concrete that lead out of the city. The ninety million little boxes that Americans travel in fittingly epitomize the breakdown of community. The transportation systems that could bring together communities of people have been left to rot and given to the poor. But as was bound to happen eventually, all the little, private boxes are getting in each other's way. What is still heralded as the fast, modern, convenient way of traveling is often as hopelessly stalled as the mass transit systems it destroyed. A society that cannot transport its people has a frightening problem of community on its hands. Conversely, a society that has little sense of community life will not even realize that a mass transportation system is at the heart of its difficulties.

The process of urbanization has led to the concentration of teeming masses of people in the urban centers. It is almost equivocal to use the word "city" for this phenomenon if one uses it as well for ancient settlements. Up to the eighteenth century, ninety-nine per cent of the cities that had ever existed were under 50,000 in population. Cities are not just larger today. The pressure of millions of people generates a new kind of psychic space.[6] Caught up in this new phenomenon that he may not even be conscious of, the human being begins to react quite differently. The bonds between people are severely tried by the contemporary urban environment.

The threat which the city poses to human community has been well explored and amply documented. Kimball and McClellan summarize it this way: "In contrast with agrarian society, in which the direct and experienced relation between the individual and his social world defined commitment, the counterpart relation in metropolitan culture is indirect rather than direct, partially rather than fully participative, symbolically constructed rather than historically experienced."[7] If this is an accurate description of the new man in an urbanized world, then we should expect trouble. One does not have to be very well informed on the latest news to be aware that such trouble is already upon us. Our surprise should perhaps be directed to the resiliency and adaptability of the human being. After all, there are only a few thousand crimes each day in New York City. Given the fact that in such a city there are several million people who are without any stable human roots, it is astounding how well most people get on with life.

---

[6] See Georg Simmel, "The Metropolis and Mental Life," in *Cities and Churches,* ed. by Robert Lee (Philadelphia, 1967), pp. 34–45.

[7] Solon Kimball and James McClellan, *Education and the New America* (New York, 1962), p. 284.

It would be senseless either to idolize or to condemn the city. Likewise, it is fruitless either to bemoan or to applaud the passing of the small town. What is important to realize is that in the shift from small town to city we will all be destroyed unless the peculiar human phenomenon of community can survive. Nothing will substitute for community, neither tougher laws and bigger jails, nor better machines and wealthier governments. Back at the beginning of our modern revolutionary period, there were already those who supposed that the millenniums-old order of human communities could be replaced by a mechanical organization. "Burke had only contempt for what he called the 'geometric' system of the Revolutionaries in which a calculated, centralized program of administrative law was set up in place of what had been a seamless web of tradition and authority, beginning in the family, rising through the community and province until it reached the king, whose rule, Burke insists, was hardly more than symbolic. The essence of the system was the individual's loyalty to the social group. 'No man was ever attached by a sense of pride, partiality, or real affection to a description of square measurements . . . We begin our public affection in our families . . . We pass on to our neighborhoods, and our habitual provincial connections."[8]

The obvious need is for a human ordering of things, that is, a situation in which the humans are in control and the things have order. Those who were fighting for a human order at the turn of this century saw no other alternative than to try to shore up the disintegrating order. Today, however, whether it is because we have more imagination or because we have reached the point of having little left to shore up, there is a great deal of talk about building new forms of human community. It should be emphasized that anyone who speaks this language should recognize what a stupendous task he is proposing. The

---

[8] Robert Nisbet, *The Sociological Tradition* (New York, 1966), p. 112.

delicate fabric of human unity cannot easily be created and must not lightly be destroyed. I am not entirely confident that humankind is capable of creating and sustaining a new order, but we do not have any choice except to try. To speak of a new era of community, therefore, is not to refer to some speculative question but to the life-and-death struggle of the human race.

Throughout the preceding material on the historical background of this issue, I have repeatedly used the word community with an implied meaning. At this point, I would like to try to make more explicit a descriptive definition of community. In proposing a definition I wish to stress the factors that have come to the forefront in this century. Although one cannot dictate that a word has only a single meaning, there does seem to be a keynote which runs throughout discussion on community. Whatever else may be added to this beginning, community denotes a human as opposed to a sub-human ordering of experience. It should be noted that a definition of community begins not with a specification of the size, purpose or location of a group, but with a description of the kind of experience an individual has vis-à-vis other persons. Some experiences make a man greater than he was, more alive, more free, more trusting and trustworthy: in short, more himself according to his own best possibilities. In contrast, other experiences degrade a person, cramp his style, destroy his self-respect, shorten his vision, dry up his love. The word community designates an ordering of human life that unites without destroying, that brings out the capacities of each individual, and that forges a bond out of strikingly dissimilar strands. Thus, community means that by meeting another person at the level of our common humanity we will share the affection and encouragement, the sympathy and the intimacy, the truth and the love, that will enable us severally to become more wholly and integrally ourselves.

A moment's reflection upon the definition I have just given will lead to the somber conclusion that this ideal of community

45

is never achieved. The ideal may seem realized between some people and at some points of time, but there is always a failure to achieve it in completeness. The closest approximation would seem to be found in the relationship of one man and one woman. But even a happily married couple—in fact, particularly a happily married couple—are aware that they do not have the ideal of community. In part, this is due to their own personal deficiencies. More importantly, however, the failure stems out of their unavoidable relationships to the rest of this grimy, struggling, and imperfect world.

At this point, Christianity can perhaps throw some light on the situation. At least it does provide some clue to the imperfection and failure of every human community. I refer to the Christian belief that there can be no perfect human communities until there is a perfect human community. Without an ultimate reconciliation to creation and the creator, man's individual projects will always be tainted with failure. The call for such an ultimate reconciliation begins to make sense in our day. The only ideal that is now worth striving after is a world-wide community in which all men are brothers. Any other way of posing the question of unity among men is simply too restrictive today. We are the first generation in the history of the world that can really think in these terms, and it is a healthy, human way to think. We are also the first generation in the history of the world that must think in those terms because our survival depends upon it. Gabriel Marcel said some years ago that our alternatives seem to be narrowing down to either an ant heap or else something resembling the mystical body of Christ. Each passing day makes his forecast seem more accurate, though the choice among the alternatives still hangs in the balance. In the previous chapter I pointed out that the era of tribalism and pre-history is drawing to a close. Here it may be added that with the advent of a world history there is necessarily a concomitant search for a world community.

Someone may object at this point: "I am not a world figure; I have enough difficulty teaching the third grade." A reply of this kind would be missing the point. What I am saying is that to pose the question of my own survival and happiness as an individual I must set the question against the horizon of a search for the community of mankind. This principle may still sound like an empty and impractical generality. Nevertheless, I insist that when community is so understood, then some things that were primary become secondary, some things that frustrate me can be borne patiently, and some steps which frighten me can be taken courageously.

Philosophers and psychologists in this century have pointed out that a unified world and a unified self are correlatives. We cannot have a world community unless we have free, integral, and autonomous human beings. Conversely, we cannot have integral selves unless we are aiming for something greater than our neighborhood, our tribe, and our nation. The reason for this does not reside simply in the fact that the world is larger than tribe or nation. To accept the whole world rather than a segment of it requires not a larger perspective but a different kind of perspective. If my vision is the tribe, then I work to defend my people against other tribes. In contrast, if my aim is the world, then there is nothing to be attacked; there is instead our common brotherhood to be discovered. The search for community anywhere will then be not for a task which will unite us but for a task which will reveal the humanity in which we are already united. Henri Bergson in his book *The Two Sources of Morality and Religion* accurately perceived this relationship: "It is only through God, in God, that religion bids man love mankind; and likewise it is through reason alone, that reason in whose communion we are all partakers, that philosophers make us look at humanity in order to show us the pre-eminent dignity of the human being, the right of all to command respect. Neither in the one case nor the other do we come to humanity by degrees, through the stages of the family and the nation."[9]

We do not come to humanity by expanding the boundaries of our neighborhood. But neither do we reach it by abandoning everything less. As a man's sense of humanity grows, his expanded vision of the universe must be accompanied by a more intense experience of the particular. In quest of the ideal of world community, one has to work with the small, fragile and imperfect realities of one's own life. We make our contribution to a world-wide unity not by amassing as many individuals as we can but by reaching out to those few with whom we can demonstrate that love is credible. One does not get to the moon by first building a ship that will fly halfway there. One begins by demonstrating in the laboratory, in the field and in the air that it is possible to get there. "The world will not become a neighborhood, even if every part of it is bound by instant communication and rapid transportation, if the neighborhood itself as an idea and a social form is allowed to disappear."[10] What must be demonstrated in an unlimited number of ways is that the human individual is not in principle opposed to the race and that it is possible for people to love each other in ways that do not imply hatred for others.

By placing the word community in this context we open the door to an astounding richness of meaning. The universal ideal becomes limitless in the possibilities it may include. The concrete realization becomes important down to the smallest detail. The quest for community becomes extremely simple; it is the search for whatever binds us human beings as human. However, the variety of forms or expressions that this quest may take becomes infinitely varied. It is crucial to make this distinction between the ideal that is sought and partially realized and the

[9] Henri Bergson, *The Two Sources of Morality and Religion* (Garden City, 1935), p. 33.
[10] Mumford, *op. cit.,* p. 146.

expression which the search takes and is constantly changing. With this distinction in mind I would like to speak about the size, differentiation and permanence of the community ideal and its expressions.

First, the question of size must be briefly considered. It should be evident from what has preceded that the size of a community, that is, an actually existing form of community, can vary from two people to five billion people. As things presently stand, a very large number of people have a difficult time trying to function as a single community. This fact does not prove that a large community is impossible, but it does suggest that work has to be done at intermediary levels to make what is available for a few people possible eventually for the billions. Most of our supposed communities are neither large enough for one thing nor small enough for another. They are neither great enough to be our future nor personal enough to be our present. This is why the small group experience is of extraordinary significance in changing the world.

Demonstration of the ideal of community has to be carried out by the fives and the eights, the dozens and the hundreds. To suppose that five or eight or any number is the ideal community would be to strip the word community of most of its meaning. A group of ten may demonstrate something that cannot be shown by two; in neither case is the meaning of community anywhere near exhausted. The small group may be a useful form of community; it may be an effective instrument and even an indispensable tool. Nevertheless, it is still not the answer; at best, it is part of the answer. The small group can provide a kind of experience and a quality of experience that are not currently available in large organizations or world government. The small group retains its validity as a community so long as it remains in fruitful tension with larger organizations.

The question of size implies consideration of the second aspect, namely, differentiation of function. There are different size groups because there are many different kinds of communities that people partake of. In the pre-industrial world, community included one's family and neighbors, one's land and work. As industrialization and its concomitants advanced, sharp differentiation occurred in people's lives. Work developed into a new pattern called the bureaucratic and it was performed in a different place from where one lived. Land, too, became differentiated from one's social group. Family and neighbors were no longer so close. Finally, the family itself differentiated into a nuclear group and "relatives." All of this development means that industrial, bureaucratic, urbanized man is a man of differentiation. This fact is not necessarily bad news. The process of differentiation can represent an advance for mankind but it does also constitute a danger. There can be an enriching of human life when it is differentiated into aspects of work and moments of play, love for the family and concern with others, a structure for efficiency and a context in which to relax. This differentiation can also destroy life for those who do not understand the process. Some men refuse to accept the distinctions and they fight for an isomorphic life which is no longer possible. Other people, instead of distinguishing aspects of life, separate their life into fragments which no longer have any unity. In both cases improper demands are made upon the communities they belong to. Thus, a man who uses his family as an aspect of work destroys his family life through a lack of distinction. The man who demands that his family make up for the rest of his miserable life destroys his family by the isolation of the parts of his life. What a man needs are other kinds of community experience that are distinct from but related to the nuclear family. Each of us increasingly lives in a multiplicity of communities. In each of them we must contribute something of what we have and in each of them we can receive something of what we need. To demand more than that of ourselves or of others is an inhuman demand.

50

It should be carefully noted that we have not gone from one community to many communities. The one ideal of community has not been multiplied; on the contrary, it has become more unified. The multiplication has not been of community but of the kinds of community expression. We have moved from a situation in which only one kind of association was possible (and this unit barely qualifies as community, since community connotes freedom) to a time when many groupings are available (and each of these groupings can be community insofar as it relates to the ideal). At one time there seemed to be a single basis for community, namely, the place where one lived and worked. Then there seemed to be a multiplication of bases, that is, neighborhood, work, social group, etc. But now we can appreciate that none of these elements is the basis for community. There is only one basis of community and it is not the primitive basis of locality but the human ideal of common brotherhood. This development does not do away with the significance of kinship, task, neighborhood, etc. If anything, it increases, their importance according to the principle that the more universal the ideal, the more particular is its embodiment. However, it situates them not as the basis of community but as changing expressions and tentative forms of the one human quest.

The last sentence introduces the final point about community, namely, its permanence. I would put forth the thesis that all community experience produces a permanent bond but that all expressions of community are impermanent. In America today, all systems are tending to become temporary, partial and mobile.[11] We have a society in which the social, political, and economic systems are increasingly *ad hoc* teams. Some people think that the situation is disastrous because there is no longer

[11] See Warren Bennis and P. E. Slater, *The Temporary Society* (New York, 1968); Matthew Miles, "On Temporary Systems," in *Innovations in Education,* edited by same (New York, 1964), pp. 437–490.

anything left to hold on to, but they are wrong. Other people think that the situation is just perfect because they are absolved from permanent commitments, but they are wrong. Both those who despair and those who rejoice make the same error in not distinguishing between people and things. Both of them fail to see that one is permanently bound to people because one is not permanently bound to things. I am not introducing a dichotomy here between people and things, only a distinction where one should distinguish. People are different from things at least to an extent, and the extent refers specifically to freedom, commitment and permanence. The challenge is to find individuals who will direct institutional flux to serve the people to whom they have a permanent commitment.

In a society of *ad hoc* teams, fidelity to people becomes practically the sole constant. More fidelity will be necessary in the future than ever before in history. The future will require strong individuals who can sustain dedication to temporary projects because they have fidelity toward human individuals. No one should be asked any more to commit his life permanently to anything, *but* all personal relationships with any depth are of their nature permanent. To bind myself permanently to anything is inhuman; not to bind myself to any people is inhuman. I refuse to accept as final any job, any role, any doctrine or any building. But I accept the fact that I am permanently bound to many people, some of whom I shall probably never see again on earth.

We are responsible for whomever we have loved. There is no escape from this responsibility. At times we may have to exercise the responsibility by going to the other side of the world. At all times we have to exercise the responsibility by using forms that are constantly changing. The world desperately needs people who will be faithful not because of kinship, location or task but because of discovered brotherhood which never ceases. The world's complex problems will not be solved by the existence of such people, but they are an indispensable resource for dealing with the problems. The Christian church ought to be one of the sources of this kind of temporary man who is sustained by fidelity but has impermanence and mobility built into the center of his life.

IV.

Community in Operation

WITH the theoretical presuppositions of the preceding chapter established, we can now proceed to a description of how the new community operates with reference to existing religious orders. I would reiterate that the word community is used throughout this book as the ideal toward which the human race is struggling. Community thus designates the most human and humanizing kind of association; it also designates the most human and personalizing kind of experience that an individual can have. What is available at any moment is a variety of limited and imperfect forms of community experience. Every community, that is, every somewhat distorted expression of community, contributes to the overall project of community. Each family, each neighborhood, each task force makes its own contribution. Each of them, however, has severe limitations. Unless challenged by more dramatic expressions of community, each one of them is liable to cease being a community at all.

There are many attempts today to create a more dramatic expression of community. For many people these dramatic forms of community will be peripheral to their lives, but for some people this kind of experience may be the center of their lives. A demonstration community is one which epitomizes or expresses in miniature the search for a world-wide community. It must have diversity and yet maintain a unity. It must uncover some of the joys and sorrows, the anger and the ecstasy, the hopes and the fears that tend to get covered over in the daily routine. The criterion for a new community is not that it be a model of unity with no human failure. The important thing is that the people are meeting at a simple human level in order to mirror a cross section of human experience rather than because they are pressured by some external factor.

The most obvious community is the family with the diversity and unity that a wife, husband and children provide. The family is sometimes overlooked in discussing community because it is not so dramatic as other aspects. The normal, stable, ordinary quality of the family is a limitation but it is also a strength. A society or a church is still heavily dependent upon the quality of its familial life. If the marriage community is in trouble then the meaning of community is in for bad times. The natural bond of a marriage and family must be cultivated and preserved if talk about community is not to become illusory.

Marriage and family run into a special difficulty in our day. As noted in the previous chapter, the family has undergone a paring down to its basic unit, the "nuclear family." Largely because of economic reasons, the contemporary family tends to be a small and isolated one. The urban family is exposed to the savage pressure of the disintegrating city. The suburban family is exposed to an isolation from the main institutions of society. At the same time that the family structure has been placed in this exposed and precarious position, more demands than ever are made upon it. Because the marriage bond is so natural and so human in the midst of a world that is often so artificial and impersonal, enormous hopes are staked upon this community. Considering the family's isolated social position, the demand may be quite unrealistic. Thomas Luckmann has pointed to the isolation of the contemporary individual and the individual's hope to cure the problem by finding a partner. "It should be noted, however, that sexuality—while a basic component of individual 'autonomy'—permits an enlargement of the 'private sphere' beyond the solitary individual and, thus, may serve as a form of self-transcendence. At the same time, it is a form of self-transcendence which remains limited to the 'private sphere' and is, one is tempted to say, innocuous from the point of view of a social order that is based, essentially, upon the functionally rational norms of the primary public institutions."[1] An individual is severely limited in his capacity to change these primary public institutions. A married couple is in essentially the same position as the individual except that those institutions will exert even stronger financial and social pressures upon them. The married couple usually finds that they must conform to the available list of choices that the huge institutions dictate.

There is an obvious need for intermediary social and political groupings that would bring the nuclear family into a relation of power with the government and business world. Tenants' associations, neighborhood groups, educational boards or political parties are attempts at filling the void. An institution that one would expect to play a major role here is the church. However, the churches, as Luckmann suggests, have never recovered from their loss of hegemony over social institutions before the modern era. Because the churches have never fully accepted a role as one among many institutions, they have fought a mostly losing battle to keep a position of dominance. When the church could no longer pretend to this position and when large numbers of churched people were fleeing the cities, the church institution went with them. It is not that the church should have abandoned the suburbs. One just wishes that the church could have done something to breach the pathological split that developed. It is understandable that the church could not stem the tide of this movement and that suburban people must now be served. The tragedy is that the church largely became insulated with other organizations that of their nature do not challenge the inhuman

[1] Thomas Luckmann, *The Invisible Religion* (New York, 1967), p. 112.

splits in our society. "At home, in the choral society, at his club, and in the congregation, he is a 'human being.' Here he is *allowed* to be man. In this amorphous, private, unregimented vacuum, in these enclaves within the industrial society, the church is also expected to demonstrate its effectiveness. With her circle and fellowships, she can fashion a Noah's Ark for the socially estranged and create an island of cohumanity in the rough sea of society which John Doe cannot change."[2]

The claim of this chapter is that there is a need for "new communities." These communities need not be church groups though one would expect some church people to be vitally interested in the issue. The availability of a variety of communities is a great need for those who are unmarried, but it remains an important factor for the majority who do marry. Most forms of community experience are short-lived, but there is a value in trying to work at community on a longer-term basis. The new community spoken of here is not the same as the community which the religious order has traditionally had. Nonetheless, there are some interesting connections between the two of them.

Religious orders might begin to find a role to play if, instead of putting patches on themselves, they would look out to the movement for community that surrounds them. They might both learn something from this movement and make a contribution to it. On the one hand, they might learn to re-examine their use of the word community and realize that it is not their own private word. They might also find that there are difficulties in the search for community which they share with other people. Finally, they might profit from some of the studies that have been done in this area. On the other hand, the people in religious orders might have something to contribute, too. Whatever the limitations of their past experience, the orders do have a long tradition to draw upon. Presumably, something has been learned,

[2] Jürgen Moltmann, *Religion, Revolution and the Future* (New York, 1969), p. 116.

if only by trial and error. The lifelong commitment that has characterized religious orders reveals much about the failings and the possibilities of human beings in community. The failings of people in religious orders are easy enough to criticize, especially when criticism is made by those who have never tried a long-term commitment. But those who are enthusiastic about community experience after a weekend attempt might learn something from people who have made a life-long attempt at it.

The following points about the dynamisms of a new community are not based upon T-group or sensitivity sessions. Much has been learned from the laboratory experience. Such workshop experiences are an invaluable contribution to the fund of human knowledge. But the group encounter is itself a compressed miniature of the more sustained new community that I am especially interested in. The source for this description of community experience is the lives of hundreds of people who have tried this kind of community living. Even the limitations and failings of their attempts should have something to teach us.

In a criticism of naïve talk about church community, Andrew Greeley has written: "It also seems not improbable that a generation of theologians will arise who will understand that 'community' is not always a good thing—that it is socially dangerous to make community an end in itself, that some communities can be oppressive and tyrannical, and finally, that communities without structure are a contradiction in terms."[3] It should first be clear that the word community is used somewhat differently in this quotation than it is used throughout this book. My use of the word community makes it *by definition* a good thing, that is, insofar as aberrations enter a community, to that extent it ceases to be a community and becomes something else. It could be debated which is the more appropriate way to use the word community, but I am more interestetd in addressing the three

[3] Andrew Greeley, *Religion in the Year 2000* (New York, 1969), p. 114.

58

dangers which Greeley cites, namely: 1) that community can become an end in itself; 2) that community can become oppressive; 3) that community will collapse without a structure. These three points must be seriously considered and a discussion of what constitutes a viable and healthy community might be built around them. This approach to communities through the misunderstanding of them may seem like a strange strategy. However, heresy is usually very close to an important truth. Badly formulated statements about community may hide some important truth that has been experienced in community.

First, it is a fact that there is a danger in trying to make community an end in itself. It is also a fact that this error is very close to the truth. If one denies that community is an end in itself, many people will assume that it is a means to an end. But to think that community is a means would be a worse error than thinking it is an end. Community simply does not fit into the framework of end and means. Part of the difficulty in discussing the notion of community is that our language and images assume that what is not an end is a means and vice versa. Thus, those who rebel against being institutional means of production see no alternative than to assert that community is an end in itself. Unfortunately, however, the result of not looking beyond the immediate community will be an estrangement from the outside world.[4] The narcissistic obsession with the experience of community may be no healthier than the role of institutional cog that is rejected. Henri Nouwen, commenting upon his experience with small groups in seminaries, writes that the team often "degenerates into a self-oriented clique in which sticky relationships drain the psychic energy of students and allow regressive behavior . . . They tend to ask for more attention than anybody can give and for more sympathy than anyone can show. They speak more about love than is healthy, enjoy in a very

---

[4] Kenneth Keniston, *Young Radicals* (New York, 1968), p. 159.

subtle way their own loneliness and show basically all the symptoms of a spoiled child."[5]

It would be naïve for anyone to suppose that small groups are the panacea for all problems. Nevertheless, there is a legitimate desire here to escape the production-means atmosphere of our world. A man ought to have people with whom he can simply relax and be himself. He needs a place where his value is not judged by what he can do but by whom he is. Most men have a home they can come to and a family for whom they are not junior executives. Most women have people for whom they can simply be wife or mother. The family thus provides a normal setting for community experience and in a way that does not become highly reflective and convoluted. Particularly when children enter the picture, the marriage partners are turned outward and are too busy with life to become narcissistic about community.

The capacity of marriage to avoid hyper self-reflectiveness carries with it a liability. Some reflective space to step back from one's role is a great advantage. Having moments to do nothing but be silent is essential to maintaining a rhythm to one's life. If mother is always doing motherly things without being able to draw support from beyond the family confines, the family eventually suffers. If father is caught in a severe economic squeeze in trying to be provider, then the family can become absorbed into the production line. The family can easily lose its own character and become the means for something else. The family, as a means for accomplishing trivial things, is demoted as it succeeds in the accomplishment; as a means for doing significant things it is frustrated as it fails to accomplish them. The family can fight back against these tendencies, but it needs the help of other communities that would awaken its consciousness of its own character.

[5] Henri Nouwen, *Intimacy: Pastoral Psychological Essays* (Notre Dame, 1969), p. 110.

The positing of new communities, therefore, is a conscious attempt to group people in a way that is neither an end nor a means. This statement will sound illogical only to those who think that instrumental and objective relationships are the only kind possible. What is still lacking in our world is an appreciation of the peculiar character of personal relationships. A person is not a means to something else; his life is not to be sacrificed to any project beyond himself. But the person is also not an end in the sense that the world does not flow into him as its final resting place. The person is not an end because he gets his identity and autonomy by looking beyond himself and by sharing the world with others. We are misled by the assumption that the person is the sum total of what he possesses and does not give away. In fact, what the person is concerns much more what he shares with others, and it is in the looking to others that he discovers himself. There is a gentle rhythm of self-possession and self-donation in which one cannot make himself a means for someone else nor can he make the other a means for himself. In a love relationship there are two people each becoming more autonomous and independent in the very act of giving themselves and in concentrating less upon themselves.

The situation of the small community parallels this picture of a person's growth in identity and autonomy. The members of the community do not gather as a means to accomplish a task. Neither do they gather without realization of the tasks that need accomplishing in the world. In order simply to be for each other, the members must also be doing other things beyond the immediate community experience. When significant things are being done beyond the community, there will not be an unrealistic demand upon the members of a community that they be the fulfillment of one's life. People then would not ask so often: Are you *really* experiencing community? They seem to imagine that there is some end point where the word community flashes on and all problems are resolved. Community provides the continuing human support which each individual needs in his search for self-worth, dignity and significance in his life. Each of the small communities that a man belongs to can provide some of the warmth of friendship and the orientation of life. None of them can go any further than that and anyone who presses the small group for ultimate solutions will only destroy its character. The small community is a by-product of people who are engaged in changing the world to make it a better place for everyone to live in.

The second point in Andrew Greeley's statement quoted above is that community can become oppressive and tyrannical. Here again, a good intention goes slightly awry. For a group to develop its own character and be a help to the members, it must exert some pressure upon the individual to leave his own shell. The individual has to trust himself to others and accept the idiosyncrasies of others. One cannot predict beforehand exactly what will happen in a small community. To enter a group, therefore, is to commit oneself to experience that may have an oppressive side to it. It may seem preferable to an individual not to belong to any group of people, but then he would have to cope with the tyranny of loneliness.

Community is supposed to deal with the problem of isolation by providing a context of compassion, understanding, comradeship and affection. For community to accomplish this task there is a minimum of intelligence, discipline and gentleness that is required. People who lack these qualities go barreling into the question of community with excessive self-consciousness, unlimited verbosity and a dangerous tendency to hug people to death. If one can recognize the isolation and loneliness in one's own life, he will refrain from smothering other people with too much togetherness. Community, it must be said once again, is not the same as a group of people always being together and talking about their community experience. Community is the most human kind of experience and as human must therefore include privacy, silence and flexibility. Anyone who does not know how to speak in silence does not know how to use words. To provide help for a person by letting him alone is what a man should learn from a community and accomplish in a community.

If people are going to stay together for an extended period of time, then they need not make life together a perpetual T-group session. People can keep some distances between themselves and gradually come to understand the rhythms and the needs of others. Because community is such a human affair it should preferably be grown into at a human pace. The fact that therapy and other special techniques telescope the experience does not mean that this is the only way or even the best way of expressing community. A calm and unhurrying pace will reveal the variety of individual needs. If some kind of peak experience is not reached today, perhaps something better is in store next week, next month or next year. Each person has his own style. Some people are not hurt by having only a short time to reveal that individuality but no one is damaged by having time and a relaxed environment to make known his person. The first appearances can be deceiving; time and gentleness do not miscalculate. "To smother with affection a person who needs but little is to force him to withdraw and become unlovely; to deprive of affection someone who needs it very much is to force him to seek it in aberrant ways. To dominate a man who is fiercely independent is as destructive as to give too much responsibility to a man needing external control. The rich capacities of each person are released for service to the degree he lives in the environment that allows the rich expression of his affection and aggression in channelled ways."[6]

The third point regarding the operation of a community is the necessity of a structure. It is true, of course, that no group of human beings can do anything together unless there is some agreement on the patterns of the operation. Nevertheless, the

---

[6] Sr. Marie Augusta Neal, "The Value of Religious Community," in *Vows But No Walls,* ed. by E. Grollmes (St. Louis, 1967), p. 165.

talk about a structureless community may be very close to the truth. If people are to be themselves and allowed to express their individuality, they cannot be fitted into a prefabricated structure. All of life cannot be so free-floating, but some of life should be. Community at its best is the experience of a break-through to a realm in which one gives and receives because one wishes to and not because the structure compels it.

In practice, of course, no one lives constantly at this level of experience. Martin Buber's "without *it* man cannot live, but he who lives by *it* alone is not a man," expresses this absorption of man in impersonal structures that are always a danger to human freedom but are nonetheless a necessity. However, to say that a community needs structure is not to end the matter. The more important question pertains to the kind of structure. Those who refer to a structureless community may in fact be referring to a structure that functions quite informally and produces little sense of constriction. There is an essential difference between being placed in a structure and being a participant in the con-tinuing creation of a structure.

In regard to the functioning of community with a minimum formal structure, the number of people involved becomes criti-cally important. If twenty-five people are trying to function as a unit, someone will inevitably end up being in charge. On the other hand, six people can live together or work together as a genuine team with each person exercising his own individual talents. Leadership will not be lacking but it will not require an official status that makes for a two-caste society. Practically all decisions can be made by group consensus and there is no feeling of being inside a structure. The structure is the people themselves and the pattern which best suits their lives. Those who deny that this kind of operation is humanly possible must ask themselves whether they have ever given it a sufficient chance to work.

This kind of community is not without its problems and its

conflicts. In fact, one of the tests of its genuineness will lie in whether it can bear differences and conflicts. Conflict is a part of human life and any social structure from which conflict is absent would have to be held suspect. The great value of the small community is that it can confront deeply human problems within a thoroughly human context. The person has the support and the acceptance necessary for facing up to what bothers him. If someone is an alcoholic, a neurotic, or a homosexual, he is not helped by being treated as an outcast. Nor is he helped by being traded from one community to another. An understanding human community is not a magical cure for any human difficulty, but it surely is an important element in dealing with a wide spectrum of problems. Even if the individual and community have to part ways, the individual may be in a much better position to face other situations than he would have been otherwise. The fact that some people leave these communities is not proof that the community has failed. It may have prepared the person for his exit to another way of life.

The claim made above that five or six people can function as a unit raises an interesting question about the differences between a community of men and a community of women. The question has hardly been raised at all in the history of religious orders. One suspects that the women have suffered by being placed into the categories devised by a male-dominated church. For me to attempt to say here what should be the peculiar characteristics of a woman's community would only perpetuate the masculine imperialism. But I would like to suggest that there are differences which need exploring.

In this regard I think that a group of six men can function as a natural unit. I am less sure that a group of six women can do so. I am not excluding the possibility that they may. I am questioning the naturalness of the group size and asking whether this should be the typical unit. At the least, I am saying that there are differences between the way men group and the way women do. In his book, *Men in Groups,* Lionel Tiger has traced the history and the anthropological basis of what he calls "male bonding." Tiger tries to show that males have always grouped together and that the bond is as natural and as necessary as the male-female bond. Men have gathered together for the hunt, for sport, for government, for war, for drinking, and for many other activities that have an aggressive aspect. "In both violent and aggressive action male bonding is the predominant instrument of organization. Females tend to be excluded from aggressive organizations such as armies where violence may occur, or even from the management of religious, commercial or administrative groups in which aggressive mastery of various environments is the condition of persistence and growth."[7] Even should one claim that the cultural bias is overlooked in this statement and that women can do and will do such work, the question remains whether a small group of women is the best and most workable unit.

It is an interesting fact that in most men's orders the word community is used with reference to the group one lives with. In most women's orders the word is used for the whole congregation. I suspect that this use of language is not accidental. What sustained men in their personal lives was a group camaraderie. Even when people in authority tried to prevent it, there was a grouping of men at a local level for a variety of purposes (including aggression against the superiors). In women's communities. on the other hand, the sustaining force was more the commitment to the ideal of the nun. There were also personal friendships between individuals but very little of a group experience at the local level.

If there is any truth to this claim, then some reservations must be raised about current movements in convent life. At least, I would like to suggest that what is assumed by many to

---

[7] Lionel Tiger, *Men in Groups* (New York, 1969), p. 171.

be *the* answer may be only one part of an answer or the answer only for some people. When half a dozen sisters move into an apartment they usually do so with great expectations that now they will finally experience community. However, once the institutional distances are dropped, people may find that they get on each other's nerves very quickly. Some of the differences and antagonisms are natural and to be expected. But it does seem that women have a tendency toward emotional conflicts beyond what men have. Apparently, there has to be a more careful picking of compatible personalities when it is a question of women. Whereas men can function as a group and replace one member of a group with another, women are very sensitive to a new personality. In a group of women there can be considerable pressure upon each individual to conform to a certain norm that is restrictive of individuality, that is, the group experience alone seems insufficient to hold the group together. The result may be that the woman has less privacy in the group than the man, while in fact she probably needs more.

The preceding remarks do not mean that men's communities can work but women's communities cannot. On the one hand, men's communities have the danger of remaining simply male groups that serve the purpose of sport or work but never get to the level of personal feelings. Men's communities may not fail badly but they may also not succeed very well because of the shell in which male emotions are kept. Men who live in all-male communities can easily develop a gruffness due to the lack of tenderness, intimacy and affection that are excluded from male bonding. On the other hand, women's communities are not necessarily out if they do not function best in the form of small groups. The failure of women's groups is not necessarily attributable to female weakness; more likely it is due to the strong individuality of the women. Community, I must repeat, refers to a kind of experience that individuals have in their association with others; and for each individual there are many communities in which the individual simultaneously participates. With a little imagination people might recognize that a far greater variety of women's communities is possible than has yet been tried. Two men do not constitute a group but perhaps two women sometimes do. A woman might even live alone and still be a strongly communal person. Who one lives with is not the only standard of one's community life. Most people apparently do not like to live alone, but no option ought to be closed as to how a woman wishes to live her life. The important thing is not the number of people one lives with but the quality of relationships that characterizes one's life.

The question may be raised about the meaning of a new community if a woman might end up living alone or living with one or two friends. The point that has to be made again is that community is not the same as one's living community. A woman with a strong sense of career and a strong dedication ought to have a variety of life styles available to her. A woman who wants a career in professional or artistic work has more need than the man for the new community situation. A single woman needs the affection and support of others lest she become the stereotype of the "career woman," that is, one who is selfish and overly dominant. A woman also needs to contribute to some projects that are larger than her own personal work. Thus, a network of communal experience and some organization to support her would all be on the plus side for a woman.

The preceding discussion about the differences between communities of men and communities of women raises a more fundamental question, namely: Should a demonstration community be composed of only one sex? Throughout the centuries, religious orders have nearly always been composed of either all men or all women. The question may seriously be raised at this time whether this is the best arrangement for the future. Before answering the question, we should bring some other points into consideration.

Religious orders up to now have been composed of people who remain unmarried. The ostensible reason for not marrying has always been that the person might love God and neighbor in a way that is not possible for those who are married. In the background, more often than not, there has lurked in anti-sexual bias. Although it is patently opposed to basic Christian doctrine, a distrust and implicit condemnation of everything connected with sex has tinged church practice. Saint Augustine had said that there is no value in virginity but only in a virginity consecrated to God. However, much else in Augustine and in medieval theology belied this position. It was easy enough to claim that one's virginity was consecrated to God and then proceed to glory in one's non-marriage status as though it were a good in itself and to look down upon marriage as though it were, if not bad, only second best.

Where Augustine and other church people were lacking was in the realization of how a consecration to God was to be worked out in human structures that include sexuality. In earlier centuries it was possible to separate people from normal human surroundings and assume that they could live an asexual kind of existence. Many people apparently did live extraordinary human lives. By whatever happy combination of factors, they did not become multilated human beings but were able to develop full human personalities.

Today the question of sexuality confronts us much more directly. Twentieth-century America may be so saturated with a sex mystique that we still do not have a healthy and balanced outlook on the place of sex in human life. Nonetheless, sexuality as a component in personal identity, as a psychological and physical force, as a quality of all loving relationships, cannot be put aside or denied. It must be admitted that religious orders have had a large number of people who never matured sexually. This fact might be taken simply as descriptive of any cross section of the human race. However, the religious orders have intentionally sought members among an age group not fully matured and then severely restricted them from contacts that would aid maturation. Now people in their thirties and forties are flocking out of religious orders largely because they discover that as love becomes thoroughly human it takes on a physical and sexual tone that is incompatible with what they have assumed to be the life of a "celibate."

It is partly for this reason that I have denied that the word celibacy has a place in descriptions of new communities and religious life. Changing the language does not cure all problems but it can clear the way for more imaginative thinking. Even if some or all of the people in religious orders remain unmarried, the word celibate is not a helpful word to describe them. I and many other people have tried to combine the words celibate and community, with heavy accent upon community. It was a valiant effort but I do not think that it works. The two words, celibacy and community, have a history which makes them almost antithetical. In Lewis Mumford's *Myth of the Machine,* he describes the 3000-year history of the "mega-machine," that is, the pyramid of war-making power, religion and authoritarian government that has characterized our civilization. Mumford claims that the priesthood of the mega-machine has always been composed of celibates because they are the perfect replaceable parts of the machine. They are expendable and submissive functionaries. Mumford then goes on to describe how the great threat to the mega-machine has always been the phenomenon of community. H uses the little band of Jews in Egypt as an example of the power of a community against the mega-machine.[8] "Ten men acting together can make a hundred thousand tremble apart" (Mirabeau).

The struggle in our world, therefore, is for community and the kind of action that will come from communal men. In try-

[8] Lewis Mumford, *The Myth of the Machine* (New York, 1967), pp. 213–33.

ing to carry through the creation of new communities, some people will perhaps choose not to marry or, if so, not to have children. But any supposed value to "renouncing marriage and sex" ought to be laid to rest. The new community would have a great advantage in having people who are free to lay their lives on the line. This kind of prophetic person has been helpful to communities in the past and there is no less need for such persons today. In this sense a man can be "expendable" in a way that reverses the expendability of the loyal functionary. The functionary does not have the normal ties of an individual. He is expendable because there is a minimum of human life to be cut off. The rebel is also lacking in the normal ties, but he has a people for whom he works and who give him support. He is expendable because he is willing and able to lay down his life for his people. This principle, of course, has always been the theory in having men free from the ties of a family in order to be free for a wider community. The instances when this has worked well may be rare, and the supposition that there should be large numbers of such people may be false. Yet there is no convincing reason why this kind of option should not remain available. The implication that marriage is the only social form that is healthy and human is a peculiarly intolerant position.

I shall return in the last chapter to the possibility of having both married and single people in the religious order. Here I would like to pursue the question of communities of men, communities of women and mixed communities that already exist. I would reiterate my principle that each person increasingly lives in many communities. Some of those communities may have one sex, others may have both. Bi-sexual religious communities have become quite common, at least in the realm of work and leisure communities. The living and sleeping communities of religious orders are practically always of one sex. If a community has only men or only women, it is obviously lacking in the diversity needed to make it a perfect demonstration

71

community. However, every demonstration community has some limitations. A community that is made up of one sex who freely choose to work at a form of community is restricted in what it can demonstrate but it can still demonstrate much. The living and sleeping community being of one sex may be the most preferable choice if the choice opens up possibilities beyond that community. Each of the individuals may be able to mix with other community situations in a way that might be effectively precluded by his establishing a marriage community.

The living community of unmarried people most likely has to remain being one sex. There are challenges to this principle coming from communal arrangements among young people today. One must be a little skeptical of the viability of such communities on a lasting basis. The religious order is perhaps realistic in having people of only one sex under the same roof if this arrangement is to be not for a weekend or a summer but for a term of years. This fact does not mean that a person in such a community should live in a monosexual world. The situation of his life ought to enable him to mix freely with people of both sexes.

A demonstration community can therefore exist if there are all men or all women in it; but it cannot exist without both masculine and feminine elements. The distinction I am drawing between man/woman and masculine/feminine is not a sleight of hand trick; it is to the heart of the matter. I wrote in *Experiences in Community* that of all forms of discrimination and repression, the suppression of the feminine is the worst. Some people thought this statement to be an exaggerated piece of feminism but they miss the point. My point does not just join hands with the typical feminist position on the liberation of women. The wider problem, as more perceptive feminist literature is aware, is the imbalance of feminine and masculine in both men and women. Discrimination against women does at least as much harm to men as it does to women. A problem that is so universal surely is the greatest single problem the race has. If someone claims that the problems of peace or urbanization are greater than the suppression of the feminine, I would answer that so long as the world is run by over-masculinized men we are going to have war and not peace; likewise, cities are going to keep falling apart until a feminine influence comes in to redesign them.

I use the words masculine and feminine in a way that is not uncommon. Masculine characteristics are hard, instrumental qualities. They pertain to the rational, dominating aspects of life. Masculinity is aggressive in its manifestations. The feminine refers to the non-rational, more personally oriented aspects of life. Femininity is receptive and accepting. This description is not of men and women but of the masculine and feminine in men and the masculine and feminine in women. Men and women differ in the mix. A man has something more than fifty percent of masculine qualities and something less than fifty percent of the feminine. A woman has something more than fifty percent of the feminine and less than fifty percent of the masculine.

Unfortunately, people are categorized into a stereotype early in life and told to be 100% little males or 100% little females. They should be allowed instead to explore what sort of mix they have biologically and psychologically. It should be up to each individual freely to develop the mix. Although it may not consciously be directed to this point, much of the revolt of the coming generation is against this outrage to people's sexual mix. The ironic thing is that adults keep saying that the young are de-sexed or uni-sexed. In reality, the young are protesting that each person is two-sexed and that they want a wider sex life than their elders. The young today are more casual about sex in bed and out of bed, between sexes and within sexes, connected with marriage and not connected with it. This attitude may sound shocking, and undoubtedly a casual

73

approach to sex has its own problems too. But a polymorphous sexuality is at least as healthy, human, and Christian as the sexual stereotype that is often opposed to it.

Religious orders probably do not think of themselves as cooperating in this movement for a wider sexuality. Almost in spite of themselves, however, they do pose a challenge to the narrowing of the word sex. If they are really looking for new forms of community they are also looking for new forms of sexuality. There is a long tradition which relates religion, community and sexuality. Those who would try to contribute to the religious life of the future must be ready to explore a new world of sexuality. What this will mean for the future is impossible to say at this time, but it does mean that no possible option should be prematurely closed.

V.

Organizing Communities

AFTER our consideration of the inner dynamics of a single community, we must turn our attention to the interrelationship of the communities. This is the question of organization or government. The consideration of government can be an unhealthy one insofar as it can bog down with all kinds of introverted details that exhaust people's energy. Nevertheless, the government of a society is extremely important. Government ought to function well and it ought to function unobtrusively so that people can get on with the important things in their lives. But many people have to be concerned with government lest it exercise a damaging influence on life.

The present chapter is the most introverted of the book because it has to set out a fairly detailed model of governmental structure for a religious order. I make no claim that the model will be useful for more than a short time, but there are a few principles at stake that are of lasting value. As the network of new communities changes character in the years to come, the governments of religious orders will change drastically. Yet the attempts now being made to create intelligent forms of government for religious orders will not have been wasted. What has been learned in these attempts will serve as models for more complex problems of unity and government.

The thesis which this chapter presents is that the religious order, for its own survival, must become a very pure form of democracy. People usually stop short of advocating this kind of government, presumably because democracy seems to be incompatible with the traditional value placed on obedience in religious orders. The word obedience is an ambiguous one: it can denote an act very exalted and virtuous, but it may also refer to a routine, functional attitude. Obedience in the exalted meaning is coextensive with the theological virtue of faith. It refers to man's most fundamental attitude toward his creator; it is the disposing of human freedom in the responsible acceptance of life. The only direct object of the verb obey in this sense is God. The obedience to God is mediated by the innumerable responses of man to his fellow man and to nature. A democratic religious order would not do away with this kind of obedience. It would encourage realization that men must obey God and not human dictators.

The exalted meaning of obedience is not the most common one. The word obedience connotes something else in our world so that it is not the best word to refer to the ultimate relation of man to God. Obedience is a functional act by which a person carries out the command of another. It is a virtue of children but not of adults.[1] Of course, adults often have to obey a specific command or rule in order to get on with life, but there is nothing especially virtuous about it. Obedience here does not consist in turning one's will over to another human being, but rather in complying with a specific command because one's intelligence dictates that this is the best thing to do in the circumstances. Human life will always include this kind of obedience, and people who do not have authority problems do not worry much about it. Nevertheless, it is desirable to reduce those occasions of life where the individual is asked to accept a decision that he has not helped to formulate. The democratiza-

[1] See "Obedience and Fidelity," in Gabriel Marcel, *Homo Viator* (New York, 1962), pp. 125–134.

tion of religious life is intended to eliminate so far as is possible this functional kind of obedience.

It is difficult to understand how one could oppose this development on the grounds of moral virtue. Anyone who would bewail the passing of an attitude proper to the childish and ignorant has a strange conception of Christian virtue. The more legitimate objection to democracy would be the classic one, namely, that in practice it does not work. Referring to this long standing fear of the working of democracies, Robert Nisbet writes: "Democracy and individualism are in relentless conflict with their own premises: each threatens to destroy what it most needs—institutional and moral props that originated in pre-democratic, pre-individualistic society. In democracy 'man is exalted by precept but degraded in practice.' The success of democracy rests upon preservation somehow of the image of man born of aristocratic society, but a whole host of forces are at work to make this impossible."[2]

The assertion that the religious order must be democratically governed refers to the principles of individual dignity, self-determination and participation in decision making. It includes the principles of organization, representation and leadership that have been found to be necessary in any large body which is not to become a tyranny of the mass. Many religious orders are trying to be democratic by doing away with effective leaders and having everyone speak on every issue at general assembly days. Whenever government supposedly changes from authoritarian to democratic over night, one can be sure that there has been practically no change. At the least religious orders ought to be aware of the inherent problems of democratic government, problems that the religious order shares with numerous other bodies today. "For better or worse now all adults must be taken into account by their governments; all clamor to be heard. Self-determination and equality are the battle cries of the century, for

[2] Nisbet, *op. cit.*, p. 284.

individuals as well as for groups that claim a separate identity. All forms of government that do not assign a formal voice to the population in their common affairs have been overthrown. Yet the democratic model also raised a fatal question: Would popular participation and freedom produce the coordination of wills necessary for asserting a polity's place in the world, or would they produce a splintering anarchy that jeopardized it?"[3]

A democratic form of government can work only if there are proper conditions. One of the chief conditions necessary is that small communities cooperate in originally producing and constantly restraining the apparatus of government. The small but effective political council is indispensable for the success of the democratic society. In Hannah Arendt's brilliant study of modern revolution, she documents the failure of revolutions to be permanent revolutions of the American kind rather than the French version.[4] She attributes the failure to the lack of small political communes which would operate within the large governmental organization. American federal government did not fully achieve the revolution, as Jefferson realized at the end of his life. In a letter to John Cartwright in 1824, Jefferson wrote: "As Cato concluded every speech with the words *Carthago delenda est,* so do I every opinion with the injunction 'divide the counties into wards.' "[5] Unless the federal government is a federation of small communities, then what is supposedly democracy will in fact be a form of tyranny.

The ideal form of government for our world is a well organized federation of communities. The religious congregation ought to be such a federation. Since it puts such high value upon community, it ought to be in a better position than most societies to carry through a democratic revolution. The religious congregation ought to be a large and strong organization not in

[3] Theodore Von Laue, *The Global City* (Philadelphia, 1969), pp. 78f.
[4] Hannah Arendt, *On Revolution* (New York, 1965).
[5] Quoted in *ibid.,* p. 252.

spite of but for the sake of the small and autonomous community. The individual needs the support and affection of a few intimates in a community setting. He must also be engaged in doing something significant. His life can be sustained only if he can believe that he is part of something larger than his small community.

The preceding remarks point both to the need for government in religious orders and the kind of government that must be developed. There is always some form of government in operation as soon as there are several communities involved. The governing apparatus may be formal or informal; it may facilitate the life and work of the communities or it may be obstructive. In any case, the matter of government cannot be avoided. The best thing that could be done is to plan intelligently the form of government that would most suit a religious congregation. That form of government is a federation. Like many other groups in the modern world, the religious order should be attempting to create a workable federation of small communities.

A federation is a tightly knit group of smaller bodies ready for action. In a federation there is agreement to vest some authority for decisions and some financial resources for action in the hands of a central authority. In this regard a federation is considerably different from a confederation which has only a secretariat of very limited powers. In his book, *The American Challenge,* J.-J. Servan-Schreiber elaborates on this crucial distinction: "The difference between a confederation and a federation is not one of degree but of kind. It can even be said that the latter is the antithesis of the former. In a confederation all decisions must be unanimous, which means that they never reach very far or very deep. Hobbled by its rule of unanimity, confederation encourages abstention rather than action, and, to use the vocabulary of economics, free trade rather than joint policies, laissez-faire rather than decisive action. If on the other hand, members of a community agree to reach certain decisions by majority vote, action becomes much simpler. Everyday experience shows that no company, trade union, club, or even family, for that matter, can function without some form of majority rule. Unanimity is a formula for negation; majority rule a formula for action."[6] A federation that is respectful of the integrity of individual communities and yet can unite these communities for action is not easily achieved.

For the difficult job of creating a federation in the religious order, there is very little enthusiasm. To the conservative the new structure may indicate a lack of order; to the liberal it may connote a lack of freedom. The old are too skeptical to throw themselves into this change; the young are too impatient to wait for the results of the change. Thus the religious order today flounders in a somewhat chaotic state. If one views the matter optimistically, it may be thought that this transition is a necessary stage of evolution. It could also be claimed, however, that the chaos is a prelude to dissolution. In any case, it may be said with some certainty that unless many people actually work at the problem of government, then there is no future for religious orders.

Many orders have put plans of government on paper but few, if any, of these orders have experientially attained a new governmental structure. This fact should not be very surprising since the experience that is required is one that will be measured in years. It must also be remarked, however, that an elaborate plan on paper combined with several years of waiting do not of themselves guarantee success. Unless people realize that there is a crucial change occurring and are enthusiastic enough to get involved in it, no progress at all will ensue.

Elaborate governmental structures intentionally or unintentionally can be used to avoid the main issue. Autocratic governments have always used impressive looking systems which guarantee

<hr />

[6] J.-J. Servan-Schreiber, *The American Challenge* (New York, 1969), p. 162.

that through a great attention to detail no fundamental changes will occur. More often today in religious orders it is an honest, unintended mistake which produces elaborate, unworkable governments. People who are constructing massive diagrams to show how the government in a religious order will work have to ask themselves: a) Will anyone read this? b) Will anyone believe this? c) Will anyone change the way he is now living? Religious orders have published so many innocuous documents and passed so many ineffective resolutions that they now have a credibility problem. Almost everything put on paper is automatically dismissed.

The attempt must be continued, of course, to put intelligent plans on paper. The change in government that is needed is a long and complicated one because it must emerge out of new experience. What is needed on paper is something fairly simple and direct that will get people into the new experience. A balance must be struck here. Sufficient structure must be provided to make the plan functional, but the proposal must not be overloaded with details that obscure the main thing being attempted.

The typical religious order in the modern world has been a minor but perfected image of the Catholic church. Its governmental operation was not entirely bad; for its own time it may have been quite good. On paper the system could get very complicated, but in experience it was quite simple. For each question there was an answer and for each decision there was a proper chain of command to follow. For nearly everyone in the system it was crystal clear at every moment what was to be done. This kind of government is usually referred to as highly centralized, though that term is misleading. It might better be called highly vertical but that term does not catch the full flavor of it either. It might best be described as a process of decision making that channeled decisions downward through individual people. The word channel is significant here; decisions passed *through* individuals. The chief characteristic of the system was neither the power at the top nor the powerlessness at the bottom, but the lack of intermediary groups.

It should be noted that the vertical line of command is highly efficient for its limited purposes. For resolving some problems it is still the best means that there is. "A series of quite simple experiments show that pervasive authoritarian modes are useful in times of crisis but more reciprocal relations between planners and workers, administrators and line and staff, are needed if the work is to be efficient over long periods of time and the workers are to retain sufficient psychic energy to continue to work creatively and responsibly."[7]

There is no great progress in letting the old system disintegrate if there is nothing to replace it. Disintegration is in fact what we have when the power to effect decisions is taken away and we are left with government by vague consensus. For example, the continuance of "superiors" in religious orders but superiors who no longer can effect decisions is neither efficient nor humanizing. It is unfair to everyone to have non-directing directors who have no real power to do anything, but who are held responsible for what goes wrong. What is proposed in the rest of this chapter is not proposed with the intention of taking power from anyone, but for the purpose of restoring the balance of power and responsibility to each individual and each group.

Nearly everyone agrees in theory to this ideal, namely, a correlation between the power to make decisions and the responsibility for action. Another way of stating this principle is to say that individuals and groups ought to participate in decisions that deeply affect their lives; only if a problem cannot be handled by those people affected by it should it be resolved by a wider authority. This principle is repeatedly affirmed by civil and ecclesiastical authorities. The fact that the principle is repeatedly violated in practice is not necessarily the result of anyone's dis-

[7] Neal, *loc. cit.,* p. 168.

honesty. The human race has yet to find the ways and means to implement this principle in social bodies. But it must continue to try.

In making the religious orders a federation of communities, the one indispensable step is to make the chapter the governing body of the order. By the word chapter I mean a body of the membership that is truly representative. Such a body must be large enough to represent the whole membership; a few members in a council or committee cannot do the job. The chapter must represent the diversity of age, work and life styles in the order. A genuinely representative body is not easily or immediately formed. It comes in the course of time from a well-developed elective process.

I use the word chapter in this context with some hesitation. Many sisters have had such unpleasant experiences with chapters in the last few years that the word has stale and narrow connotations. Nevertheless, I chose to use the word because it is one with a long and rich tradition and one whose exact meaning is still flexible. It is also the word that is in theory closest to what I am referring to, that is, chapters are supposedly representative bodies. As a matter of fact, nearly all recent chapter bodies have been highly unrepresentative, but this has been due to deficiencies in the elective process that can be corrected. The word council might be a good word to refer to the representative body, except that in most orders council has a definite and narrower meaning. A provincial council in a religious order nearly always means a council of the provincial's instead of a council of the province. An assembly, in contrast, usually has a wider meaning than chapter and might best be retained for reference to meetings of the entire province or region. Thus I come back to the word chapter as one whose salvage should be attempted for the specific purpose I am describing.

Many orders have started electing superiors, splitting up offices and appointing committees. Although these changes may improve the present exercise of authority, none of them dramatically does the thing that needs doing, namely, a reversal of the movement of authority. What must be affirmed and demonstrated is that human authority arises from below and that it is vertical only because it is first horizontal. Making the chapter to be the governing body effectively accomplishes the reversal. It is only in this way that there is removed from the religious order the most objectionable of authority situations, that is, one man's person being at the arbitrary disposal of one other person. A diversification of power does not guarantee avoidance of error, but no diversification inevitably leads to some people being harmed by power.

I have said that the chapter must be large enough to be truly representative. The phrase "large enough" can only be defined by reference to several criteria within a particular situation. The most important factors are the level at which a body functions and its relation to subsidiary bodies. For example, the United States Senate has only one hundred members to represent two hundred million people. If this were the only representative body, it would obviously be too small. The Senate could be representative, however, not only because of its relation to the House of Representatives but also because of intermediary bodies such as city councils and state legislatures. In a religious order that is national or international in scope, there may be a place for a senate or council at the top but only on the condition that there are strong regional chapters.

At the regional or provincial level, the order should function as a very simple federation of communities. Its governing apparatus should be close to the people. As a general guideline it could be recommended that the size of a regional chapter be one-fourth to one-sixth of the members. To be larger than one-fourth would usually be cumbersome. It is also unnecessary because the participation of the majority should be through the power of the vote, the use of communication media and the forum of general assembly days. To be smaller than one-sixth would tend to remove the government too far from the people. If a region is a federation of communities, then each community ought to have at least the possibility of representation. The average living community, I am assuming, should soon be about six people. If the chapter is one-sixth of the membership, then it would be possible for each community to be represented. I am not talking here about how the election should be conducted, but simply about the size of the body. The election should be run in a way that guarantees a diversity of age, interests and life styles.

The one-sixth proportion of representation may produce an unwieldy size. For example, if there were six hundred people in a province a chapter of one hundred would probably be awkward. The solution, however, may lie in the direction of reconstituting the provinces in smaller groups rather than in diminishing the proportion of representation. In any case, the numbers cited here are not to be taken rigidly. In all questions of government there are more important matters than number. All questions of numerical size should be open to reconsideration in light of other factors.

The chapter as governing body must meet regularly, presumably at least once a year. At the start of its operation, two meetings a year may be necessary. If the chapter functions properly, it should not be necessary to extend its sessions beyond a few days. The chapter should ordinarily function through the subsidiary structure it creates for itself. It should meet only on the business for which it has been thoroughly prepared. A sure indication that a chapter does not understand its own nature is chapter sessions of weeks or months. A long meeting may be necessary to constitute the body; the question of what a chapter is should be the main agenda of the first meeting. Once it has taken a decisive step toward discovering its own power and nature, it should adjourn. The continuing work should be carried on by a small number of standing committees and a varying number of *ad hoc* committees.

As a working model I would suggest that a chapter might have four main committees: 1) work 2) community 3) training 4) finance. Over a period of time it may be found helpful to divide some of these committees. For example, it would probably be a good thing to split a committee on work into a group on present commitments and another group on new projects. Likewise, the issue of professional training might best be divided into preparation of new members and advanced training or retraining of older members. Nevertheless, it is best to begin by making these groups subcommittees within standing committees. If it is found that there is a clear separation of interests, the two subcommittees could then evolve into standing committees. In general, it is preferable to change a subcommittee into a new committee rather than vice versa.

I assume for this discussion that there are only the four committees listed above. It is the responsibility of the four chairmen to see that business is brought out of committee for action by the chapter at its meetings. The chapter should have a chairman elected by the chapter. The chairman's job is mainly organizational. While a chapter is in session, the chairman should be assisted by a committee on procedure. In addition to the chairman I would suggest one other job, namely, the office of coordinator of committees. This role is one of being a watchdog or a whip. Some people may think that this job represents unnecessary bureaucratization. It is true that the job cannot be well-defined beforehand and perhaps the chairman could handle these duties. Nonetheless, it might be better if the chairman is a calm and methodical operator concerned with the overall organization and functioning of the chapter. For the coordinating role there is needed a person who can put some pressure on others, cut through procedural delays and see that workable proposals are brought to the floor.

Distinct from all of the offices within the chapter is the role of president. The president of the region should be elected by direct vote of all the members of the region. It is his job to approve and implement the decisions of the chapter. For this purpose he has the choice of ratifying or vetoing the chapter decisions. His veto can in turn be overridden by a two-thirds majority of the chapter. The president is the executive officer and does not legislate. However, he may propose programs to the chapter committees for their consideration.

The way in which the president interacts with the chapter is the most critical question of the whole structure. If the analogy of federal government were followed, we should create a separate executive branch and provide the president with his own council or cabinet. At this moment of evolution in religious orders, this expansion of structure around the president would not be helpful. The president as executive officer has a distinctive role and sufficient influence. His relation to the chapter provides enough of the element of check and balance. Instead of developing his own cabinet, he should work with the four committee chairmen, the chapter chairman and the coordinator as his council. These seven men form the council that oversees the region, meets regularly and exercises the effective leadership. The president can be advised, of course, by any number of people, including people outside the order.

The relationship between the president and the chapter has to be worked out in practice. Perhaps the biggest danger is that, unless the chapter is sufficiently strong willed, all power will be assumed by the executive. This alignment will occur not because of an executive seizure of power but because the chapter does not experience and assert its role. Councils, committees and chapters could remain what they nearly always have been, namely, a rubber stamp for one man rule. It is for this reason that I stress that the decisive change must be the assertion of power by the chapter. No one can give it power beforehand and no one can really take it away once it has been assumed. The question is whether everyone, including present superiors, can see that this move is for the good of the whole order.

Partly to dramatize the limits of power on each individual office, I would not make any office a full-time job. This suggestion may be very naïve; undoubtedly present superiors in religious orders would think so. However, when the president does not have to visit each community, negotiate contracts with bishops or dispense permissions, it is conceivable that his job could be a part-time one. If government by representative council can be achieved, it would be best for everyone if no one is a full-time superior. So long as any one person is appointed in charge, decision making power tends to drift to that person. Government of the group by the group ought to be given the fullest opportunity to work. Mother houses and provincialates could quickly cease to exist. In this way of operating, the leaders of the order need not give up the work for which they joined the order. It would simply be that for a period of perhaps three years part of their work would be to function in the leadership team.

It should be obvious that the role of the chapter is not to "give permissions." No one needs permission for his own inherent rights. Every individual has the right to receive the training he needs, to work where he can best use his talents and to live with those whom he wishes. Of course, every individual, whether in or out of a religious order, has the exercise of these rights defined and qualified by his social environment. Thus the chapter has as its role the expediting of individual choice and the improving of the social environment. In practice a chapter may have to be a limiting factor, but it must always be seeking to limit its limiting role. For example, the function of the committee on professional training is not to assign people to study. People decide for themselves when, where and what they wish to study. However, at present there may be a conflict of responsibilities in religious orders. Existing contracts and financial situations may conflict with the desires of many people to do further study. For a few years it will be necessary for some body to reconcile conflicting responsibilities. Two points need emphasis in this regard. First, the institutional commitment should not automatically take precedence as has usually happened in the past. Detailed procedures ought to be set forth which show respect for the individual's choice as far as is possible. If the individual is asked to postpone his choice, it ought to be clear to him why and for how long he will do so. Second, the chapter committee is to eliminate itself from this role as soon as it is feasible. It is not to take to itself the power formerly held by the provincial. Its role here is the transitional one of transferring the power of assignment from the superior to the individual.

The long-term work of the committees is twofold: first, to provide information and services not easily accessible to the individual and the communities; second, to commit the region to projects that cannot be undertaken by an individual or a community. The first function is important but fairly routine; it would not draw much opposition from anyone. The second function is of more central concern and would be looked upon skeptically by many people. The issue must be faced squarely because this is the point at which one must decide between federation and confederation. Only the former, I have maintained, is an organization for action, because it has authority to decide and money to act. The government of an order must have power or else there is no order.

Many people will be dismayed by the suggestion of a government that can make commitments for the region. Their experience in the past makes them wary of anything that smacks of mere slot-filling. It is true that so long as there are institutions there is a risk of dehumanization. Yet the elimination of institutions is not the only alternative, not even a possible alternative. Despite the difficulty of the task, there is no worthwhile alternative for the human race except to try to build institutions which humanize rather than dehumanize, that is, organizations which are supra-personal instead of infra-personal. With strong individuals and good organizations, institutionalization can enhance rather than destroy freedom.

Freedom is not attained by liberating men from organization. The first step on the road to freedom is the liberation from internal and external bonds of slavery. The second step is the effective commitment of oneself to something worth living for. If a man cannot love and work in effective and efficient ways, then his freedom is abortive. Thus the full exercise of freedom requires organization, government and leadership. People in religious orders who have suffered under repressive authority may think that freedom consists in eliminating authority and letting each individual go his own way. Freedom would then be understood to be the absence of any institutional restraints upon a person. However, the destruction of institutions for the sake of freedom is a myopic policy. Somewhere and at some time institutions have to be changed to protect and support human freedom.

The suggestion here is that the religious order is a good place to try to create a supra-personal organization. The job is a tricky one, always needing more effort and constantly exposed to failure. Nonetheless, the religious order still has the possibility of doing things that no individual and no small group of people can do. Admittedly, its way of doing things in the past often turned people into a means of production. But with a reformed government the institution of the future can be put at the service of individual freedom.

A religious order could, for example, establish an urban training center to provide religious and other kinds of educational services for an area. The work would be established because there was a sufficient number of people ready and willing to engage in the work. The order's length of commitment and its extent of financial involvement would depend on many factors including the interest of all the members in the region. No individual would be assigned to the work or subtly coerced into working there. Commitments ought to be flexible enough so that the work would be there for those who wished it, but if eventually no one wished to do the work, then this particular work would cease to be. There is no sense in an order trying to duplicate all the institutions of civil and ecclesiastical society. It should create those institutions that it really wishes to have and are not available elsewhere. Teams of well-trained professionals who do not need much money are in a unique position to take on whatever jobs need doing.

It may sound utopian to presume that individuals can do just what they wish, while the organization can still maintain efficient institutions. In practice there will always be conflicts and pressures, bad investments and inflexible arrangements, irresponsibility and selfishness. The possibility of the ideal and the actuality of the failings both point to the need for an intelligent, democratic government that is in touch with all of the people. A government of the people by the people does not immediately guarantee that all institutions will efficiently serve the will of the people; but no other form of government or lack of government has any chance of success at all.

The concept of organization is inseparable from that of leadership. New organization demands a new kind of leader. Warren Bennis defines the new form of leadership as follows: "An active method for producing conditions where people and ideas and resources can be cultivated to optimum effectiveness and growth. The phrase 'other-directedness,' unfortunately, has taken on the negative tone of 'exclusively tuned in to outside cues.' For a while I thought that 'applied biology' might capture the idea, for it connotes an ecological point of view: a process of observation, careful intervention, and organic development."[8]

[8] Bennis, *op. cit.*, p. 119.

91

The times are very puzzling for leaders who have been schooled in a different concept of organization and leadership. They fluctuate between laissez-faire policy and occasional panicky interventions.

The role of the leader is not dead; it is more necessary than ever. The leader of the future must be a man who understands the human roots of power. He must know how to create conditions that will unleash that power. There is no longer any need for the kind of leader who is judged efficient because he gets everything done by himself. Although inefficiency is by no means the ideal, it may be preferable to the kind of efficiency that is in opposition to imagination, creativity and team work. The ideal leader is the one who is strong enough to keep turning power back to each person at his own level. The next best leader may be the weak one who unintentionally brings other people to make decisions for themselves. The worst kind of leader today is one who is only partially incompetent. He works diligently at being a good leader, which is perhaps the worst way to be a leader.

To those people who are not sensitive to the peculiar character of *human* power, all of this may sound like gibberish. Inhuman power is greatest when it is a dominating external force. The leadership that pertains to human power is an inspiration born of confidence in the force of personality. If a leader knows who he is, he will be less anxious to mold other peoples' lives and more intent on letting them find out for themselves who they are. An Eastern sage once wrote: "The wise man when he must govern, knows how to do nothing. Letting things alone, he rests on his original nature. If he loves his own person enough to let it rest in its original truth, he will govern without hurting them."

The ideal leader is ceasing to be the domineering one who can frighten people into submission. What is needed now is the low-keyed personality that is strong enough to reject the trappings of office. He must be the kind of person who is willing to survive by the resources built into the human being. He will refuse to lead by giving orders and he will refuse to be honored because he holds an office. Good leaders do not just fill an office. They stamp their personalities upon the office so that the office is never again the same. Religious orders can best do away with "superiors" by putting some people in office who refuse to play superior.

The new style of leadership was well described by Prime Minister Trudeau of Canada. Asked by a reporter how he was bearing up with the responsibilities of his office, he replied: "I increasingly feel that this important function, this great authority that is called Prime Minister, actually does not exist. My ministers and I are men like others but particularly adept at the framing of questions. We then seek their answers with the rest of the world . . . It is above all essential that everyone participate, that each has a feeling of responsibility and the desire to convince or be convinced."[9]

In a group of people who freely decide to live together in faith and to work together in dedication. such a conception of leadership should be possible and appealing. Religious orders that are currently establishing new forms of organization have at the same time a marvelous opportunity for developing new leadership. All that remains for the order is to find this kind of leader who can put the order on this kind of road to the future.

[9] Quoted in Servan-Schreiber, *op. cit.,* p. xxiii.

VI.

Work and Community

RELATED to changes that are taking place in the nature of community and in the nature of organization is the change in the meaning of work. The theme of work is the third topic which we must address in the search for a new form of religious life. As with the two previous chapters, this one will be a blend of principles applicable in the whole society and suggestions for those who are currently in religious orders to move in the direction advocated here. I am concerned with how the nature of work itself is changing today and the consequences of this for people interested in new communities.

Freud described the healthy person as one who could love and could work. The word as used in this way seems to connote something more than drudgery or "earning a living." Work would seem to constitute a basic component of human existence; it is one of the things that life is for. If this be true, it is puzzling to read that work is going to disappear. In thirty years, it is claimed, only a small number of people will work, and they will work for only a few hours a week. Whether or not this prediction is realistic, it indicates a confusion about the nature of work and the kind of society we are trying to create. This is a question that cannot be postponed until the next century. We have already passed a highly symbolic mark, namely, for the first time in history more than half the people in our society are in "services" and less than fifty percent are needed for making "products." This statistic is not very meaningful, however, until we investigate further the kind of reality designated by the words service and product.[1]

A few reflections upon the relation between community and work will be helpful in examining the meaning of work and the new forms it is taking. I mentioned in Chapter IV that a community is not a group organized to perform a task, that is, it is not a means of production for work. On the other hand, a community is illusory unless it faces up to the relationship of its members and itself to the world of work. There is a subtle interrelationship here which is often overlooked by people who in rejecting the "rat race of the American institution" enthusiastically embrace the experience of community. People who decide against working from nine to five and going up the ladder of the business world sometimes trust in community as an alternative. What usually happens when such communities are launched is that after a good start in which people "really love each other," the community experiences a slow disintegration. The more intently the members look at themselves to find a cure, the worse things seem to get. For one thing, the economic pressures can bring down the whole project. Money should certainly be secondary to other considerations of community. Nevertheless, without a minimum to survive in a way that is not dehumanizing, the difficult task of establishing new communities becomes overwhelming.

My use of the word task in the last sentence indicates the ambiguity involved here. In one sense the main task of a new community is simply to be a community. However, to be a new community means to look outward to the building of mankind. The main task of the community is to be a community but it must, as it were, concentrate attention not on its primary task but on its secondary tasks. The secondary jobs (e.g., teacher,

[1] See Peter Drucker, *The Age of Discontinuity* (New York, 1969).

doctor, social worker, etc.) feed into the major task of being a community by enriching the life of each member and by keeping the community looking outward. If the community tries to be itself without working at tasks beyond itself, it becomes disengaged from the world and contorted back on itself. This statement is not a condemnation of monasticism, which when it is strong never loses an "engagement" with the world of man and nature. The man who goes out into the desert, wrote Thomas Merton, had better be going there to find his fellow man or he will not find God or himself. One should remember that there are more ways to engage the world than by rushing in to help people who are in need and whom we suppose need us.

Instead of plunging into work as the way to cure all problems or, conversely, instead of rejecting work as useless, we should examine carefully the meaning of work and its relation to community. We should neither substitute work for community nor take community to be an alternative to work, but we should see that these two are inseparable components of a life that is fully human. It is the relationship between these two components that is causing so many problems today. By clarifying their relationship, the nature of work will be better understood and the quest for community will not strangle itself. The latter is a distinct possibility when the most ardent advocates of community approach the subject with a strong anti-institutional bias. Somehow our institutionalized world must be transcended and perfected beyond itself and not simply negated. Work, humanly understood, is the means by which this is to be done.

In *Experiences in Community* I pointed out that there should be a distinction between a person's community life and the organization needed for work. There should not be a separation between the two but rather a distinction in unity. Without the distinction there is a blurring of the conditions that should exist for each. I have strongly criticized religious orders for their failure to develop the kind of organizational structure needed

for work. The failure has resulted in a covering over of inefficiency and incompetence with a false kind of personalism. What
is supposedly kindness and charity can be a cover to hide the
need for clear-cut professional conditions. Persons can be helped
to flourish as persons when they are protected and supported by
many impersonal mechanisms. I have strongly advocated that
religious orders make use of the efficient means by which
American organizations have progressed, that is, the bureaucratic pattern. What follows may seem to contradict this point,
but I am only trying to carry the point one step further. There
is a moment when one must emphasize the distinction between
community and work; there is another moment when one must
emphasize that the distinct elements are united. The latter point
pertains to the new era of work, which I refer to as post-bureaucratic.

Commentators on business, education and government organizations have begun to speak about the end of the bureaucratic
era and the emergence of a new form of organization. This
new organization will characterize the post-bureaucratic era. I am
always skeptical about anyone using the prefix "post." It is a
cavalier way of dismissing problems and answering critics to
proclaim oneself as post-Christian, post-ecumenical or post-mod-
ern. One could doubt that we are post-anything. With great
reservation, therefore, I am using the phrase post-bureaucratic
to characterize the direction of American organization. The contention is that the future lies with this form of organization even
though most organizations are presumably not now working on
this basis.

As I have indicated in dealing with community, bureaucratization was part of the larger process of urbanization and industrialization that has occurred and is still occurring in the modern
world. Different parts of the world are at various points on the
time line. Thus a country in which technology has only recently
begun to play a role may still be trying to organize a bureau-

97

cratic pattern for its work. Most American corporations are bureaucratic, although many of them are trying to go beyond simple bureaucracies. They are trying to introduce motivations, environments and social relationships different from those that typify bureaucracy. Universities are confusing places these days because they waver uncertainly between pre-bureaucracy and bureaucracy. The university is a monastery taken over by a corporation. It would like to pretend that it is both one, big, happy family like the monastery and also an efficient production plant like General Motors. However, the students know that the whole university is as confused as they are as to what it really is. I have already indicated where the religious order is on the time-organization continuum, namely in the pre-bureaucratic pattern. During the last century it did not undergo the process of bureaucratization that affected most organizations in America. This fact does not necessarily condemn it, but it means that it must carefully examine how it stands in relation to other organizations and where it wishes to go from here.

Bureaucracy is a development in organization which enables it to deal efficiently with large projects. It is a system of functions and authorities that combines the strength of human skill with the accuracy of mechanical precision. Bureaucracy divides people in terms of work hours and non-work hours. While the person is at work he need not worry about being a good person but only about being a good worker. People are further subdivided into the skills they possess. Some people become "hands," other people are the "brains" of the organization. Likewise, the work to be done is also divided into simpler elements. When the elements are parceled out to cooperating individuals, jobs can be done that would stagger the imagination of pre-bureaucratic man. There is a direct line traceable from Ford's workers rolling the first model T off the assembly line to the thirty-four thousand men cooperating in the landing of the first man on the moon.

98

Bureaucracy is a word which describes a stable and efficient way of organizing people for accomplishing some work. In popular usage the word bureaucracy is almost entirely negative in meaning. What people think of bureaucracy is perhaps best indicated by the immense popularity of *The Peter Principle,* a satirical essay on the workings of bureaucracy. There is reason for this bias against bureaucracy, although its strengths and values should first be appreciated. Bureaucracy's chief characteristics are its insistence upon conformity to the rules of the system, its appointing of a superior who is given power in order to obtain compliance, its clear allocation of rights, duties and responsibilities. These characteristics give the system its strength and stability. Where there is need for methodical, prudent and disciplined work, bureaucracy will probably always be unexcelled.

The stability of the bureaucracy, however, can work to its own undoing. In a time of rapid and unexpected change, the set patterns get in the way of creative adaptation. Robert Merton has described this built-in limitation of bureaucracy in a series of four steps by which an efficient and useful system of action becomes a rigid and stubborn obstacle to change.[2] First, the maintenance of the system requires a high reliability of response. The rules must be emphasized more than the minimum necessary to assure the response. Second, a strict devotion to rules leads to their absolutization. What had been the means to some further end begin to be treated as ends in themselves. Third, the concentration on keeping the rules of the system interferes with the need for adaptation to changing conditions. Each bureaucrat, concentrating on his own little domain, will oppose radical change in the system. Fourth, the elements that lead to efficiency in general lead to inefficiency in specific instances. At the moment when imagination is needed, the bureaucracy finds that imagination has been excluded as too dangerous. The

[2] Robert Merton, *Social Theory and Social Structure* (Glencoe, 1957), p. 200.

strength that makes bureaucracy efficient for its limited purpose makes it vulnerable to anything new. As J. K. Galbraith pithily summarizes the matter: "A bureaucracy under attack is a fortress with thick walls but fixed guns."[3]

Besides its incapability to make rapid change when needed, bureaucracy has other objectionable features. Technology and bureaucracy seem to bring in their wake an obsession with production and with the quantity of goods available. Almost all effort is expended on achieving *more* with little regard for the quality of human life or the quality of anything else. Furthermore, the enjoyment of all these goods has usually been reserved for a minority at the top of the hierarchy. The gross national product expands, but the lot of the workers does not dramatically change. Relative to the top of the society, the problems of the poor seem to grow worse. Lastly, the parceling out of human beings and their control within an impersonal system do damage to the delicate structure of human community. As has been pointed out, work was to be separated from community and function on a different basis. However, life is not that neatly drawn and people insist on putting themselves back together. As they achieve a sense of self-determination in other areas, they begin to find intolerable their treatment within a bureaucratic work structure. Both DeTocqueville and Weber had foreseen that although bureaucracy and democracy were born of the same dynamism, they must eventually collide.[4] The moral imperative of democracy impels us to look for a way to organize groups for work other than the bureaucratic way.

A new form of organization is now in the making, an organizational pattern that I have called post-bureaucratic. Such organization will try to retain some of the main gains from bureaucracy, such as its efficiency. At the same time, it will try

[3] John Kenneth Galbraith, *How to Control the Military* (New York, 1969), p. 68.
[4] Nisbet, *op. cit.,* p. 148.

to recover some of the elements too casually put aside in the rise of bureaucracy, particularly the need of the person to determine his life as a whole. Such an organization would break through the rigid pattern of bureaucracy and become "patternless by excess." It would not be lacking in structure, but the structure would be personal rather than impersonal and would emerge from a new crystallization of community within work itself. Beginning in the 1940's, studies on worker motivation revealed the importance of environment, management's concern for the worker, and *esprit de corps* of the work team.[5] Ever since then, a slow transformation has been occurring in the work pattern, and a new attention to the human side of things has characterized American organization.

A fully developed post-bureaucracy would do away with all the rigid formalities of bureaucracy. As a result, the pre-bureaucratic and post-bureaucratic superficially resemble each other. For example, in both forms the person's work and home life are closely tied together; in both forms the person plays more than one work role. The important difference is that in the post-bureaucratic a differentiation has occurred and a new unity has been achieved which does not obliterate all distinctions. The point can be illustrated by considering the evolution in formal education. In the pre-bureaucratic, a teacher is a person who teaches his children in his home while he also grows food for the family, makes furniture for the house, etc. In the bureaucratic era, a teacher leaves his home to go to a school where he does nothing but teach during his work-day hours. In the post-bureaucratic stage, the home and school come back together. Teaching will be what nearly everyone does as part of his interests. In the future it will not always be evident what is a school and what is not a school, who is a teacher and who is

[5] See Lester Coch and John French, Jr., "Overcoming Resistance to Change," in *Readings in Social Psychology* (New York, 1952), pp. 474–491.

not a teacher, when education is happening and when it is not. Although the third stage resembles the first stage, there are enormous differences. In the third stage, the family does not take back what once went to the school. Instead, the school breaks down its walls and goes out to people of all ages wherever they are. Environments of learning made possible by technology will enable people to get the sophisticated knowledge they need for living in a complex age. It is not the parent as jack-of-all-trades who must provide the education but the many specialists from all walks of life who will discover that teaching others is part of their specialty.

The post-bureaucratic will therefore require better organization and more careful planning than the bureaucratic. The artist who does things by forgetting about rules has to work to the point of getting beyond rules. The spontaneity of human beings is maintained only when the conditions are planned that make spontaneity a continuing possibility. To enable people to be whole again in a complex world will require expert organization. There is no going back to the "simple world" of the pre-industrial era. There is no resting place in the present complex era. We must push forward to a "simple complex world" where the complexity has been understood and integrated. The bureaucratic pattern is a good development so long as it is transitional to something better. What is certain is that bureaucracy gets in its own way unless some people work to perfect organization and transcend bureaucracy.

I have said that the religious order is mainly pre-bureaucratic. It may pride itself on having some of the qualities that characterize the post-bureaucratic, but this appearance is illusory. An order which has not changed much from its beginnings is pre-bureaucratic, not post-bureaucratic. In trying to become post-bureaucratic it must be careful not to short-circuit the process and pretend it has arrived at the end when it is barely struggling through the beginning.

The religious order in some respects seem to be highly bureaucratic, but this is also illusory to a large extent. Although bureaucracy has things like strict rules and superiors, it does not follow that wherever there are rules and superiors, there is bureaucracy. On the contrary, to have rules and superiors without the prior framework of a differentiation of person and function is to have the worst of both worlds. I mean that bureaucracy allows a superior to command obedience solely because it first specifies that this power applies only in clearly defined segments of space and time. Bureaucracy can treat a person impersonally without destroying him because everyone first agrees that the person's dignity and life transcend this system.

In sum, the religious order is neither a well developed bureaucracy nor a post-bureaucratic organization. When the order seems to have elements of both, they are in the wrong place. The order lacks bureaucracy where it should be, that is, in its work structure, while at the same time it carries bureaucracy into a person's living community where it should not be at all. Thus it has a little bit of everything but in a crazy-quilt pattern. The adaptations it has belatedly made have not been thought through on any consistent basis. "The religious community has taken on the style of bureaucracy in its own form of operation while retaining the mass-elite orientation to the people in high office and the pervasive affection and obedience expectation of the parents in the old matriarchal-patriarchal patterns of tribal and peasant days."[6]

Before the religious order can enter its post-bureaucratic phase, therefore, there is much that it must learn from the bureaucracy. For example, each person in a religious order ought to have a work contract that spells out the condition of his work, the responsibilities he has, and the remuneration he will receive. It astounds me that religious orders are still not generally doing this. A work contract is "merely bureaucratic" and should even-

[6] Neal, *loc. cit.*, p. 153.

tually be surpassed, but before one can claim to go beyond, one must get so far. The more successful one is in his work, the less important do things like contracts and money become. However, it should first be clear to people in bureaucracies that the worker is post-bureaucratically willing this. If a person in a religious order has the talent and training to be earning $15,000 a year, he should have a contract to be paid that amount. The person who does not need or does not desire that much money can reinvest eight or ten thousand dollars of that salary back into the work. Because he believes in what he is doing and is interested in more important things than money, the service he offers will be far in excess of what the institution need pay and perhaps can pay.

Anyone familiar with Catholic institutions will recognize this financial arrangement as similar to the one that has made these institutions possible. The one crucial difference is that each person would be treated as an individual with his own rights and duties, whereas the present system operates on agreements between diocesan officials and religious superiors. The current system confusedly combines pre-bureaucracy and bureaucracy. People are placed into institutions to work before there is an unmistakable acknowledgement that they are free, adult human beings. Even as a money-saving device it simply is not working anymore, and yet the only thing done is a dragging of feet to slow down the perilous rate of change.

The alternative, I am suggesting, is that each individual in the religious order be recognized socially, economically, and politically as a free agent. When religious begin to get access to the particular kind of freedom which the bureaucracy provides, they may decide to leave the order. But that is happening anyway. The hope that the religious order must have is that people will see that bureaucracy is only a stepping-stone to a post-bureaucratic pattern. This latter might be found inside the religious order as well as outside it. All that would be needed is that a sufficiently large number of people from the orders be willing and able to create the institutions they want. Some of the people who are free enough to leave religious orders are also free enough to stay so as to work in association with others.

At the present, it is important for each individual to have the kind of working situation which respects his personal dignity. The religious order ought to insist upon the minimum protective devices that have grown up with bureaucracy. However, I do not think that we should have to go through fifty years of bureaucracy before coming up again on the other side. There is a sense in which one must go through the same painful experience of learning that someone else has had. Nevertheless, there is no need to repeat all the mistakes previous people have made and to follow the same history of development. For example, when European catechetical leaders come to this country, they almost invariably give the impression that they understand our problems because they went through this phase twenty years ago. They go on to imply that in another twenty years we will be up to where they are today. Even if the first point is true (which I doubt), the second point does not follow at all. The thing to do in such movements is to use the short cuts that the other group had to learn by trial and error. In this way one can find paths that may save years or centuries. An earlier phase of development has strengths which it should apply in leading, instead of blindly following someone else's route of progress. To follow through with the example: American catechetics, instead of relying on the native instinct for freedom, experience and organization, tried to import a prefabricated message from Europe. That phase never succeeded very well. But now by concentrating on our strengths we could, despite a lack of scholarship, soon be ahead of rather than behind the European countries.

One must work with bureaucracy, therefore, but not place much trust in it. Religious orders have to use bureaucracy today, but they should do so warily and with an eye to avoiding unnecessary encumbrances. The religious order is in an interesting position with regard to the passing of bureaucracy. Orders have been underdeveloped organizationally, which has been a bad thing. Ironically, however, this deficiency can be turned an advantage in the attempt to create new organization. Bureaucracy is a transitional pattern, but it inevitably gets in its own way. The religious order in the work side of its life does not have the internal resistance offered by an immobile bureaucracy. There may be some autocratic personalities in the way, but they are passing from the scene in the normal process of times. What the religious order most has in its favor is a large number of intelligent and dedicated people. They could create an adult, efficient, post-bureaucratic organization. What they need in order to do this is a thoroughly democratic process with the kind of leadership proper to representative democracies. There is obviously a close connection between the capacity of religious orders to generate new government on the one hand, and new work structures on the other.

The preceding discussion was necessary befor trying to answer the question: Should individuals in religious orders work on their own, or should there be a corporate work of the order? The word "corporate" is a highly ambiguous one in this question. There is, first, a kind of corporateness that is implicit in the pre-bureaucratic stage, and that is supported by bureaucracy. Corporateness at this stage springs from the lack of individuality among members and the infra-personal character of the institutions that direct them. People who ask the question about corporate commitments usually have this meaning of corporate in mind. A corporate action here means that everyone works in the same building on similar schedules under the same code of rules. The alternatives to this corporateness seem to be either chaos in the institution or a splintering of the group into individuals with their own isolated domains.

The suggestion of this chapter is that there may be another

alternative to mass collectivity on the one hand, and laissez-faire individualism on the other hand. This is the second meaning of corporateness, the one proper to the post-bureaucratic era. In this instance, a group of fully individualized people decide to cooperate on a project. For their purpose they create a supra-personal organization, that is, one that, while not diminishing individuality, can do more than any individual on his own could do. Certainly, our world needs people working together rather than in isolation. The work team is the ideal which is replacing the bureaucracy. This is a more effective corporate activity because the individuals contribute not just functional efforts but their own individual talents.

Bureaucracy creates a body of people that are united, but they are not united as people; the union is created through bonds that are sub-personal. The person who refuses to work in that kind of institution may be anti-social, but it is also possible that he may be more social minded than the bureaucracy allows. He may be looking for corporate activity that strengthens individuality rather than opposes it. "The well designed production team represents in microcosm precisely the kinds of relation that we would call one of commitment. First, each person has a determinate role in the team, a role he can perceive as an indispensable element in his own self-concept. Second, this role, which has been shown to be more than a technical skill, is recognized in the group as performing a function. Third, the work of the team as a whole is disciplined and supported by objectively defined purposes."[7]

The religious order is an obviously suitable group of people to experiment in this kind of corporate organization. The sense of community that inspires their lives should carry over into their work where community is regaining importance. The somewhat unstable and impermanent character of such organizations should not be a great hindrance to them; it should be something

[7] Kimball and McClellan, *op. cit.,* p. 266.

of an advantage. A highly trained specialist who has strong community support and no fear of economic security can have extraordinary leverage. There is no shortage of things to do that are urgent, dangerous, and poor paying.

The economic problems should not be what frustrates religious orders. It is absurd that this factor prevents them from doing all the things they could be doing. There should be more than enough money not only to give full support to the work of each member but to provide for training and retraining of people in any skill. Anyone who has been working in a religious order for the last ten years ought to take a year off to think, to read, to travel, to study, to learn a new trade. The suggestion is not an unrealistic one at all. Everyone in society ought to get a sabbatical leave, but the great majority of people find it economically and socially impossible. The people in religious orders can start the process immediately, especially with their middle-aged people. The claim that it is not economically possible to do this is false. Any economic policy is feasible if all the alternatives are more expensive. The religious order that is losing the young in whom money has been invested and that is letting the middle-aged die on their feet and become economic cripples, is fighting a losing economic battle. The order ought to allow everyone to study who wishes to study and encourage some to study who need it but are hesitant to begin it. If necessary, the order should borrow the money to get through a stage which is temporary. A group in which most members can earn two to five times what they are now living on, simply does not have an economic problem. Its problem is the political one of realizing that it does not have to operate this way, and of therefore implementing policies for living in a new way.

Considering the new forms of education and social work now emerging, the religious order should be in an excellent position. It can simply open its doors to the work world about it. As soon as it gives up its privileged ghettos and begins to participate fully in the city life about it, it will find no lack of demand for the many services it can render. In fact, a danger in this move is that people rebelling against segregation from others are liable to think that the new ideal is to be always involved with others. Activism in one's work life often springs from a lack of community or family that one can turn to for support and relaxation. It must be emphasized that the post-bureaucratic organization, although it brings community and work back together, does not obliterate all distinctions. An open community does not mean that it is open day and night for problems of work to come spilling into the lives of people who need moments of leisure and privacy.

Many groups from religious orders who have moved into urban ghettos have tried to solve all of the problems of the neighborhood while working at other jobs as well. This super-dedication quickly leads to total exhaustion, which is a help to no one. If work is going to be done with a surrounding local community, it had better be done in a manner that is competent and allows some privacy. In a book that is very sensitive to the need for a more personal kind of education, Harold Taylor can still write: "There is a point at which a teacher must stop short and say to himself and his students, I am a teacher with a life of my own, you are a student with a life of your own, and although we share a number of interests and should spend a generous amount of time together in fulfilling them, there is an inviolate part of myself and my life which is neither yours nor the university's. It is my own and I will not allow it to be completely absorbed by committees or responses to protest."[8]

The particular difficulty in which religious orders in America find themselves is that they are tied to a school structure which has worse problems than they do. The popular mind has so closely identified the problems of the religious order with the Catholic school that it is assumed that one must go down with

[8] Harold Taylor, *Students Without Teachers* (New York, 1969), p. 298.

the other. There is evidence to suggest that this is what is occurring, but neither the downfall of the Catholic school, the dissolution of the religious order, nor the interdependence of the failures is inevitable. Unfortunately, a less than imaginative approach to both situations makes the problems of one rebound on the other. For example, if there are fewer religious in a school, the tuition is raised for the students. As the tuition is raised, it drives out the economic group that the religious orders might best serve. As the schools begin to serve the people who least need this service, the young religious who are the backbone of the operation get discouraged and leave it. Then the cycle begins again. The astronomical tuitions now being charged in diocesan schools guarantee that the schools will be at the service of a tiny minority that will be economically, socially and racially segregated. The claim of dioceses that the high tuition is necessary to continue the schools is a sane remark based on insane presuppositions. It begs the question of why a diocese should be in this business at all. The contention that this system is serving the church and society as a whole becomes more preposterous with each tuition increase.

My remarks are not intended to be an attack upon the concept of a Catholic school. As many commentators inside and outside the church have remarked, some variety and competition in education could be a good thing. A school that would be truly catholic in vision and interest would be able to experiment and to change rapidly in ways that a public school will probably never be able to duplicate. The present policy of trying to stretch a thin system thinner not only does not work but it also prevents the emergence of a new catholic school. My generalization may seem unduly harsh since one could cite exceptions to the rule. Nonetheless, there has been no concerted move in the system as a whole, and that is the issue here.

If some Catholics wish to get together and run their own school, it should be their right to do so. A diocesan structure could perhaps help them to get their project initiated. If anyone wished to send their children to such a school, it would be up to them to pay the going cost which might be $1000 or more for each student. Such private schools already exist, including ones run by groups of Catholic lay people. The educational significance of those schools may be limited, but there can still be a commitment to excellence for those who want that kind of school.

There is another kind of school that the religious order should best be suited to handle. In education which is more informal, which operates from a community base, which serves those not well off in the society, the religious order has an obvious place to work. If the diocese will not support this work, then the order should take it upon itself to establish such schools from its own resources and from resources of other agencies. Such education should be available free or at a nominal cost. The school or quasi-school would be run almost exclusively by people in the religious order. Anyone else who joined them would do so because he was able to afford a contribution to such a project and wished to work there.

There should thus be complementary kinds of schools for different segments of the population and administered by clearly defined groups. Instead, there is presently confusion of purpose, unhealthy competition, and a failure to serve the people most in need. Religious orders once dominated nearly every school in the system. In time the orders could not staff the schools and as a result lay people were somewhat reluctantly brought in. The attitude has never really changed much, if only for the simple reason that the laymen cost more. But the struggle to keep a high percentage of religious in the the schools and the consequent difficulties of laymen negotiating for a just wage do not make sense. The schools are in the process of losing their *raison d'être* and the religious, laymen and general population are no longer being served by such an operation.

111

The point of this discussion is to suggest a way of action for religious orders. The suggestion is one that is already operating on a small scale but needs rapid, clear and dramatic enlargement. Religious orders ought not to close any more schools. They ought instead to disengage themselves as orders from the entire system of Catholic schools. This does not mean that members from religious orders will not continue to teach in existing Catholic schools. Presumably, many men and women will wish to do so, at least for a while. It should be up to them to decide which school they wish to teach in and to negotiate a contract with the school administration. It is fairly obvious that many schools where no religious wish to teach will have to close their doors. The decision to close is up to the local community and the officials responsible for the school. This move may exercise a hardship not only upon Catholic groups but also in the public sphere which may have to supply alternate means of education. The hardship is being worked anyway, and this proposal would at least make a little clearer what is going on.

When a religious order these days announces that it is going to close a school, there is inevitably an outcry from that part of the population being served by the school. The result very often is a paralysis precisely when decisions are urgently needed. If the order as order simply dropped all commitments to the school system, then the decision would be placed in the proper hands. A local school board could decide to keep the school if there were sufficient interest on the part of the community, sufficient money to hire a good staff and the means to run a good school. The religious order for its part would be freed of the lead ball that is dragging it down. Its people could stay where they are if they liked. But they could also move at will into new work sponsored by the order or engaged in by the individual on his own.

The religious order is only one potential wing of a movement to carry education back into the center of community life. The

112

rumblings, conflicts and experiments in education have been described in many recent books. The movement is still small, but if it draws upon that power of community experience described earlier, there is no limit to the power that might be generated. Particularly with the help of communication media today, small teams of people who are well disciplined and know what they are doing can influence the whole country. George Leonard may be exaggerating when he writes that "with educators, parents and students looking for new approaches, six radically different—and successful—schools could transform education everywhere."[9] Nevertheless, he has a point. Even if only a minute percentage of those who are in religious orders were willing to try, those few could be enough to alter the Catholic church in America.

[9] George Leonard, *Education and Ecstasy* (New York, 1968), pp. 219f.

VII.

Religious Community in a New Era

In Chapters II and III I described the ideals of religion and community that are emerging in the society today. In the last three chapters I have suggested some changes in existing religious orders that would bring them more into line with these broader currents of religion and community. It remains now to suggest some further steps to be taken and to predict some of what might occur in the birth of a new form of religious community.

An issue that might first be raised is whether the kind of change advocated here is compatible with the religious life tradition of the past. It can hardly be denied that there is an immense distance between the monasticism of centuries ago and the kind of religious community being described here. It should not immediately be presumed that the change is all downhill. The claim can be made that the new religious community is more genuinely representative of Christianity than was early monasticism. Without condemning that early monasticism, it may still be said that its good effects were achieved in spite of some aberrations of form and some misguided principles.

Christian theologians, I have previously said, had an impor-

114

tant point to make in claiming that Christianity tries to break through the category of religion. Theology perhaps overstated its case inasmuch as Christianity in most respects resembles other religions. The fact that they are empirically similar, however, does not exclude there being a dynamism inherent to Christianity which reverses much of the meaning of religious doctrine and practice. A sociological approach that neglects the underlying principles of Christianity might construct a framework for treating "religious community" that is logically consistent but mostly inaccurate.

If the ambiguous meaning of the word religious is not kept in mind, the wrong meaning may be associated with Christianity. An ideal of "religious community" may then be assumed which is almost the opposite of what Christianity should imply. Kenneth Westhues has done an historical and sociological study entitled *The Religious Community and the Secular State.* His assumption is that the most religious community in early Christianity was the one that separated itself from the "this worldly." Successive stages of development can then be understood only as compromises with secular forces. He writes: "A few further remarks, however, may be made about this prototypical religious community. It was, above all, characterized by otherworldliness. It intended to stay as far away from bureaucratic church and sinful world as possible . . . Life was an unchanging routine of the unpursuit of earthly goals through penance and mortification, and the pursuit of God through contemplation and prayer, with a little time begrudgingly given to the work necessary to grow some food so that one could live to suffer more."[1]

The same author goes on in a like vein to describe what the ideal of the religious man is: "Because his consciousness is occupied so steadfastly by the dream of what is perfect, the religious person refuses to compromise his attention with the in-

---

[1] Kenneth Westhues, *The Religious Community and the Secular State* (Philadelphia, 1968), p. 44.

numerable short range goals which day-to-day life in the world presents. He is typically unconcerned with money, with people's opinion of him, with his clothing and diet—with all the things that are for most of us the goals for which we work and the delights of which we dream. Passing these dreams by, the religious person concentrates on the dream of unity, of timelessness, of no more separation of people from people, of no more death or pain. His is a cloudy, nebulous dream, because it is so far removed from the world of today."[2]

One gets the impression from statements like these that the author is not only giving a more or less accurate description of early monasticism but is also putting forth Christianity's ideal of the "religious man." There is no suggestion that this ideal represents the false religion that Christianity is opposed to. This concept of the religious man has always been a dangerous enemy for Christianity. The reason for its being so dangerous an enemy is because the ideal can superficially appear to be the one that Christ preached in the gospel. However, the statements cited above are filled with ambiguous phrases that are weighted in the wrong direction. Christ, it is true, did not "compromise" with immediate goals of everyday, but he did go around healing the sick, comforting the sorrowful and siding with the outcast. There is a dream in the biblical tradition, but it is not cloudy and nebulous; it is taken from the most concrete images and experiences of man. The kingdom of God is not something far away in the "other world," but something springing up in the midst of mankind where the Spirit is transforming man's flesh.

In short, there are two ideals of religious community and they are diametrically opposed. One is anti-Christian even though it has often appeared in the churches. The other is affirmed by Christianity at its best, and affirmed by many other traditions as well. The former opposes the "this-worldly" to the

[2] *Ibid.,* pp. 24f.

"other-worldly"; the latter overcomes this opposition. The first assumes that there is a conflict between man's concern for life in this world and religion's concern or another lie. It deals in the abstractions of short-range goals versus long-range goals, ordinary facts versus dreams, work versus contemplation of God. The second ideal recognizes that the greatest enemy are the very abstractions used to pose the previous oppositions. It realizes that the aim is not to choose long-range dreams over short-range concerns but to find a way of being so deeply immersed in the present that a dream of the future is awakened. It does not deal in abstract moral principles; the moral teaching of Christ, C. H. Dodd once wrote, is "embarrassingly concrete." Opposition to the prophets did not arise from their concern with the other-worldly. The reason that the prophets did not fare very well was because they stubbornly called the neglectful community back to a proper care for this world. The "religious minded" who avoided the world because it is sinful were special targets of the prophets. It was Jesus, most of all, who reminded men that all creation belongs to his Father and that the world with all of its people is not to be rejected by his followers.

Both kinds of religious community are at odds with what the majority are usually attending to. It is easy enough to lump together these opposite movements. There is a marginality to the right and a marginality to the left. Some people are different from their society because they hate it and wish to escape it. Some people are different from their society because they love it and wish to transform it. The former group combines self-righteous idealism and strict asceticism to produce a separated sect.[3] The latter group combines a flexible program and a gentle

---

[3] Kenneth Keniston ("Moral Development, Youthful Activism and Modern Society," in *Critic*, 28 [Sept./Oct. 1969], p. 24) makes the interesting observation on the present youth revolution that the lack of asceticism among youth can be a hopeful sign. Revolution is most dangerous when it combines self-righteous idealism and strict asceticism.

discipline to produce a community that cares for the world. Those who do not flee a sinful world do not necessarily deny that there is sin; they may face evil in a far more radical way and see it even in themselves. The choice is not between being for the world or being against it. The difficult task that the gospel urges is to be for the world in such a way and to such an extent that one can subsume within this affirmation a negation of all that is wrong. Love bears within itself a passionate hatred. Christ's principle of being in the world but not of the world has nearly always been interpreted in a crude and simplistic way. Actually, Christ was very subtly playing off one meaning of world against the other in a way that keeps love and hatred locked in constant dialectic.

It would be easy to extend the typology of the two kinds of religion, both going under the same name but one directly opposed to the other. Enough has been said to obviate objections that the religious community should not get too involved with the world. An incarnational religion simply cannot be too involved, although it must constantly examine what it means to be involved. The ideal of the "religious community" in Christianity is to uncover a way of life that is more integral for the person and more concerned with the quality of human life.

The problem that looms large is the feasibility of any attempt to create such "religious communities." Recently, Erich Fromm concluded a book by calling for the creation of a network of communities across the country.[4] He even invited the reader to fill out an entry blank to join one of these clubs or groups. He maintains that a few hundred people would be able to have an enormous impact on the whole society. "Whether or not there are enough people who wish for a new form of living, and are strong and serious enough to form such groups, I do not know. Of one thing, though, I am sure: if such Groups existed, they

[4] Erich Fromm, *The Revolution of Hope* (New York, 1968), pp. 157–169.

would exercise a considerable influence on their fellow citizens because they would demonstrate the strength and joy of people who have deep convictions without being fanatical, who are loving without being sentimental, who are imaginative without being unrealistic, who are fearless without depreciating life, who are disciplined without submission."[5]

Hardly anyone would deny that such a network of communities sounds like a worthwhile project. Yet the difficulty of beginning and sustaining such a movement is enormous. There has to be a cultivated soil of tradition if things human are going to have much chance for survival. In such undertakings one could also use a few people who have had long experience at the task. Even if they are quite imperfect people, they have very likely learned some invaluable aids to survival. The suggestion of this book is that religious orders in the Catholic church now have or recently have had a large fund of such people. Even should one suppose that the great majority of people in religious orders should not be there, there would still be an enormous number in comparison to all other new communities.

As important as the people now in religious orders is the number of those who have recently left an order. Often, these people are still interested in a community experience and dedicated work. It practically always happens, however, that these people leave one by one. Having no economic backing, they are quickly caught in a financial bind which has the effect of isolating them. Great hope is constantly expressed that new forms of community will grow up among people leaving religious orders. Little success has been realized because the obstacles are so great. Efforts have to be continued in this direction, but a much greater sustaining force will be necessary. The religious orders could still take a role of leadership in this movement. Whatever their faults, they do have organization, tradition and numbers in their favor.

[5] *Ibid.,* pp. 166f.

I come back here to a question touched upon several times already, namely, the value of large numbers. People constantly misunderstand the question of size. There is a great deal of opposition both within and without religious orders to large organizations. Several politicians running for office in recent national elections have used the theme that they are opposed to bigness. Many people in the country seem sympathetic to this position. However, to be against bigness is a quixotic position. The universe is big, the earth is big, the country's population is big. How is one going to fight these and a thousand other big things?

The enemy of the individual person is not bigness but something quite different. It is the isolation of the individual and the feeling of powerlessness in the face of growing complexity. The individual's problem is not something's bigness but his own helplessness. What he most lacks is communal support that would give him a base from which to interact with the large organization. Failing to grasp this fact, the individual flails wildly at the large organization and the authority figures at its head. If by any chance the leader is brought down, the individual will find himself just as helpless as before. Dictators come and go while the masses remain a mass. All the power goes to the top because of the lack of organization at the bottom.

The growth in size of an organization does worsen the position of some individuals insofar as it will make unfree people more unfree. On the other hand, people who are well balanced and self-determining will have problems with the large organization, but they will not feel suffocated by it. If people experience a communality that provides love and vision, then giving these people institutional bigness for support increases their power. The experience of intimacy with a few human beings is a necessity for human growth, but it is not a sufficient basis for human life. We desperately need large organizations of autonomous adults who can break through the privatized sphere into the world of primary social institutions. A well-governed organization of 10,000 is in all respects stronger than an organization of 100 or 1000.

The religious order ought to be a place where large organization is less of a threat. At the base of its structure lie not isolated individuals but communities of free adults. At least, this is theoretically the case. Religious communities in practice often did not supply the affection, intimacy and support that the individual needs. Now when there is a discovery of "community experience," there is often a concomitant disaffection for any large organization. This is a dangerous point of development because just when the large organization could finally become an alley, it becomes the butt of attack for people seeking community. A sister who says that her order is too large to reform has missed the point. Size may be one of the few things it has on its side. A disintegration into small groups is occurring in religious orders, but though the novelty is at first refreshing, there is no long-term future in this change.

One reason for the splintering into small groups is the conviction that the world view of several groups in the same order is too diverse to maintain a unity. Existing religious orders have such a difference of outlooks in them that it seems sensible to admit that the split exists and to formalize it. Some orders have already divided into two new orders but not with entire success. The attempt to divide a small order may worsen the situation because the order does not have a sufficient number to give it stability. An order derives much of its stability from the tradition it is rooted in. It is more difficult to create a new tradition than to do away with an old one. A lack of tradition can be partly offset by organization and large numbers. A small order, in trying to overcome its problems by splitting into two, will probably fragment into many pieces, none of which can hold together.

The desire to realign religious orders according to world

view is probably a legitimate one. I would suggest, however, that before they divide they should first amalgamate. Perhaps it is more realistic to hope that the two processes of division and amalgamation would go on at the same time. As a diversity of life styles is being introduced into existing orders, a phasing out of the differences between orders should also be occurring. In time there might develop, on the one hand, a network of religious houses that will try to maintain the monastic and conventual tradition of the past. On the other hand, another network of communities might gradually jell into a national federation.

The distinctions between religious orders are today not only useless but detrimental. In a stable social situation, competition between groups can be stimulating. Dominicans striving to outdo Jesuits perhaps had some point to it a few centuries ago. But when a society is fighting for its survival and identity, competition fragments unity and wastes energy. There is no logical reason for the multiplicity of orders. The reason traditionally given, namely, that each order has a specific calling ordained by providence, can hardly be sustained. The more likely cause of origin in most cases has been that it seemed easier to found a new order than to reform the existing one.

People are still trying to found new religious orders. It is an attractive but illusory way of trying to cure the problems of existing orders. In the case of the churches as a whole, the conviction has finally come about that an ecumenical movement is the best policy. To reform the church by founding one's own sect is no longer a viable policy. Somewhat analogously, the person who is interested in religious community had better be cautious about doing it by founding his own order. The same very human problems will show up almost immediately in any group of people, no matter how carefully the people are picked.[6]

[6] See E. Schein and W. Bennis, *Personal and Organizational Change through Group Methods* (New York, 1965), pp. 107–113.

Existing religious orders have no monopoly on frightened, insecure people.

In most orders today there is a sizeable number of people who are fearful of any changes and feel incapable of making major adjustments in their life. There is another sizeable group who are looking for a more dynamic community and flexible organization than are available today. An amalgamation of orders would present some threat to those who want no change, but the threat would be compensated for by the consequent strength of the new order. The other group would then be freer in having financial and organizational backing together with a fair amount of consensus in the community life form.

I do not have a blueprint for implementing this change. I suspect that it will be considerably easier to bring about unification when religious habits have disappeared. Perhaps some large orders should simply absorb small ones. Unfortunately, the large orders do not yet have the organizational flexibility they need to accomplish this job. The joining together of small orders is a possibility, but unless this is accompanied by other moves in a larger framework it probably will not cause much of a strengthening. Perhaps the switching from one order to another will become more common. If a sister is not appreciated in her own congregation, there is no evident reason why she should not be able to switch to a different group. A final possibility is that small groups from several orders could cooperate in establishing an American religious order. For such a project to be successful, however, it would have to be a well coordinated move by several hundred people. The tactical difficulties of such a move would be enormous.

The most hopeful sign on the horizon is the development of councils of religious, usually at a diocesan level. The formation of such bodies already accomplishes a transcending of individual orders. Gradually, the leadership of these councils could effectively replace the superiors who are supposed to lead the separate congregations. The active cooperation in various projects may lead to an obliteration of the differences between orders. A merger might take place similar to recent ecumenical mergers among Protestant churches. But the development of a helpful super-organization does not come about automatically. It requires hard work on the part of someone.

One great danger in the formation of *diocesan* councils is that they will be taken to be part of the diocesan structure. Sisters' councils are often advocated as a parallel organization to priests' senates. The use of the priests' senate as a model for the formation of sisters' councils would be disastrous. It would strengthen the illusion that diocesan officials are the controlling agents of religious communities. The secular priest is directly subject to his bishop. Whatever may be the kindly intentions of the bishop, the secular priest is exposed to arbitrary decisions over his whole life and work. A priests' senate, not exactly as a labor union but fulfilling many of the same functions, protects the rights of the individual priest and gives him the support of his fellow priests.

A council of religious has a quite different reason for existence. It is a joining of religious communities so that they can better decide and more effectively accomplish whatever they decide for themselves. The council of religious is not an extension of the local bishop but independent of him. Religious in the country should not always be in opposition to the bishops, but they might on occasion be in fruitful tension with them. A council of religious might negotiate with the diocesan authority over the conditions of work in diocesan institutions. A bishop should have no more to say about the inner workings of a religious community than about the life of any Christian family.

It is unfortunate, therefore, that religious councils are being established on the basis of dioceses. These councils are liable to strengthen what they should most be breaking down, namely, the illusion of monolithic power in Catholicism. Realistically, however, there is probably no other place where this development is going to begin. One must make the best of this situation. At least the religious ought to be clear in their own minds about what they are doing. They ought to realize that the ideal is to break through the diocesan pattern and create a national movement that will be out in front of the official church. Sisters who are now being offered the same rights and responsibilities as diocesan priests might think a while before accepting the favor. What they should be looking forward to is the emergence of trans-diocesan structures and national leadership.

If an amalgamation of orders into one or several movements were to occur, then a split into various life styles could be sustained. Not only would there be distinct life forms but there could also be a variety of ways of belonging to the movement. The continuance of an organized movement requires a corps of people who stick with it and do most of the organizational work. Other people may join in it for a few years and then move on to something else. I would stress that the main thing advocated here is not "temporary vocation" but a redefining of *in* and *out*. If a person has built up friendships and working relationships with members of the religious communities, there is no reason why he need ever be considered *out*. A few of those who now consider themselves "alumni" of religious orders might value some association with the order and be able to give it some help. In the past this was probably true of only a small minority of the "alumni." But today many people leave with no sense of bitterness, alienation or "loss of vocation." They feel they must try things on their own, but most of their friends are people who were or still are in the religious order.

This change of situation indicates that religious orders should make provision for close association with former members. However, something more fundamental than that may be called for. Why cannot the religious order be flexible enough to bear far more diversity than it has now? Some of the old traditional

125

orders might be in the best position to open their doors and start a vital religious life movement. Eventually, they could merge with other sprouting movements that have all of the advantages of flexibility but all of the disadvantages of rootlessness.

It is particularly in the large cities of America that a religious life movement could serve an obvious purpose. Patricia Sexton, describing the difficult straits of the American woman, writes: "No society has yet explored the possible variety of urban communities. Yet it is in the city that the weakest nuclear family and the greatest need for community exist. The rapid decline of the various forms of solidarity in the city: religious, ethnic, political class—even nationalistic—intensifies the need for new communities."[7] There already do exist in cities thousands of communities of sisters. Convents could open their doors tomorrow and take in young women who are new and alone in the big cities. Many young people just out of college and starting a professional career would appreciate a place to live that offers companionship, privacy and low cost. In all likelihood, such people would remain for only a year or two, but there could be mutual profit from the brief stay. The people in convents would have to face up to their own human situation in a way that is not accomplished by a thousand hours of intramural dialogue. The young person would receive some invaluable assistance at a transitional period in life. Occasionally, the young person might establish a permanent relationship to the religious community.

All kinds of difficulties can be cited in order to show that the preceding suggestion would not work. It must be admitted that the difficulties are real and that there is no predicting all the effects of such a move. A young woman accepted into one's home could turn out to be a delinquent, and this could be awkward and dangerous. However, if the community were strong enough, there could be a good result from such a happen-

[7] Patricia Sexton, *The Feminized Male* (New York, 1969), p. 160.

ing. A young woman who has gotten into trouble may be the one who most needs help and could most profit from this kind of help. The question then is whether the nominal community is an operative community that could meet the challenge of giving personal help to someone who desperately needs it. The community must certainly examine itself to gauge whether it has a minimum of stability of its own. If it can begin to offer help, it might just find that it will receive more of a life for itself in return.

It is important that such a move not change the community into hotel keepers. If some people in religious orders wish to run a home for transients or wayward girls, there may be a great value to such work. What is discussed here is something different, namely, the taking of an individual into one's personal community life. To keep the distinctive style of the community and yet have an open door policy is not easy, as both rural monasteries and inner city communities have discovered. That does not mean that the attempt is wrong or that it necessarily causes chaos. The policy can be implemented if it is done intelligently and with the realization that what counts is the quality of a few relationships that are being sought and not the quantity of people who are supposedly going to be saved.

Lurking behind the other tactical difficulties of this proposal is the threat which it poses in the sexual sphere. The young person temporarily living in the religious community would presumably wish to bring home dating partners. As most religious communities now exist, the entrance of the "other sex" is a problem. The fact that a girl bringing her date to dinner at a convent would be awkward only points up the need for changes in the structure of religious community. A person ought to be able to bring home his or her friends. This is not possible, of course, when the religious community is not a home but a hotel. In a hotel one tries to control sex or at least keep it out of sight. In a home sex is not considered a "problem" but the normal texture of life. When one's community is a few other

127

people who have agreed to share life together, then the bringing in of one's friends becomes a normal pattern that adds to the life of the community. One cannot deny that steady dating between young unmarried people tends toward marriage. If someone who is temporarily with the community is courting before marriage, the others in the community ought to be able to rejoice with the person. Even if someone who is supposedly *in* the order is considering marriage, the other community members ought to be able to accept and support this development. Why cannot a religious community support a variety of relationships and courtship instead of immediately putting a person *out?*

The answer that will probably be given to the last question is that religious orders are made up of celibates and that as soon as they get interested in sex they should in all honesty leave the religious community. Whatever may have been true in the past, these distinctions are not as clear cut any more. With the changing patterns of sexuality and community, particularly in the metropolis, the religious community cannot avoid the changes as if they did not exist. Unless the religious community can face up to the question intelligently, it is living in an unreal world.

The sexual area is where the religious community encounters its greatest threat but also its greatest opportunity. At the end of *Religious Community and the Secular State,* the author writes: "If the enjoyment of sex comes to be considered among Catholics of secularized society as an interpersonal expression of love which may or may not result in children according to the particular goals involved, it is difficult to understand how the utilitarian justification for celibacy upon which so much emphasis is currently placed can win the support of sufficient numbers of religious idealists to keep religious communities in existence on a large scale."[8] The curious thing about this statement is that the opposite conclusion could be drawn just as well.

[8] Westhues, *op. cit.,* p. 119.

As the nuclear family becomes less the absolute standard, the religious community will begin to have a more "utilitarian" reason for existence. If people who love each other are not intending to raise a family, then there is no need for them to leave a religious community if they are in one, and considerable reason for them to join one if they are not there. The religious community makes sense precisely for people who wish to love and to work in a way that will help them to avoid being isolated. People who are not bringing up a family are in special need of community to give a context to their love and organization for their work. Whether some people should be called married or unmarried may be difficult to say. The exact nature of their relationship will be up to them to determine. In any case, I have insisted that the word celibacy does not apply to anyone in a religious community. With its historical overtones of sexlessness, celibacy is a word that has an anti-communal bias built into it. Community and sex go together. This does not simplistically mean that community can only be achieved in bed, but it does mean that man's bodiliness (including sexuality) is intrinsically related to his sociality. A community which brings out all aspects of the human must have the tone, excitement and dynamism of sexuality.

Some people will read into these lines all kinds of dark and strange forebodings. There is no intention here to hint vaguely at a secret program. The vagueness in what is proposed springs from the nature of the subject and the confusing period in which we live. We have broken through a Victorian code of sexual ethics but we have hardly emerged into the clear light of day where people would generally understand their own sexuality and live sexually in a responsible way. Women have been liberated by law from a secondary place in society but in fact the liberation is still in the early stages. What effect this change will have on sexual mores is impossible to predict. What the human race will decide to do with its energies when some of the cultural inhibitions dissolve is also impossible to foresee.

What can be said with certainty is that new communities will be desperately needed that will allow for a diversity of the human while supplying a personalizing love.

The question of whether there could be married people in religious orders, therefore, is probably not a radical enough question. The question is usually asked out of a narrow context which assumes that nuns are clergywomen who could also solve their problems by marrying. There are several erroneous assumptions behind the question. Liberal reformers who seem to suggest that people in religious orders could get married and that everything else could remain the same are extremely naïve. Religious life as it now exists and marriage as it now exists have opposite dynamisms. The logistical problems of keeping a unity to these two forms of life are staggering. However, one should not drop the matter at that. Marriage very likely will rapidly change in form. Religious orders could begin changing their patterns to the extent that some married people might be said to be within the order.

I must stress once more that the point of these proposals is not to get people in religious orders married, as if that were the ultimate salvation. The problem in our society is not that some people are unmarried but that the word sex is, for married and unmarried, so narrowly understood. Sex needs to be reintegrated with *eros* and with the spectrum of human attitudes toward work and play. When sex becomes a tone of all bodily encounters then it will bring people into communion rather than isolate them. The aim, therefore, is to get to a community life that would truly be sexual because it would include young people interacting with old people, single men with older women, married men with single women, men with men, women with women. To presume that any of these relationships is precluded by a marital relation is to accept the narrow social and economic framework that is forced upon most people today.

130

Children would, of course, be a key question in any move of this kind. A large number of children would usually put a great strain upon the cohesiveness of a tightly structured community. On the other hand, some children may be a welcome contribution to a community larger than the nuclear family. It should be recalled here that being in the same community does not necessarily mean living under one roof or in the same apartment. The important thing is that a social bond be developed that would give each individual greater religious, political and economic power.

The religious community of the past has usually maintained existence by the composition it kept. Adults of the same sex living in a tightly structured system excluded all those disruptive tendencies toward sexual expression and children. No one should be so naïve as to think that these dynamisms can be casually introduced and unobtrusively absorbed into the former framework. The old wineskins are going to burst anyway and the question now is whether something new can be created. There is no reason why communities of adults cannot be receptive to much more love and sexuality; not that this will happen easily but at least it is socially realizable. On the other hand, it is doubtful that a federation of communities can include many children without a break-up of the groups. At least, this would seem to be dictated by the social and economic conditions of the present. One of two directions could be taken from here. The number of children may decrease with people reproducing the same number as themselves rather than adding to the total population. This development seems likely in the so-called advanced countries where information and techniques of birth control are readily available. The other direction which is more unlikely would be the developing of a kibbutz system for rearing children. This system is a neat and simple one because it allows the adults to concentrate on the bonds of adult community. The children, as they are brought up in a communal setting, develop

131

their own kind of society. There are many unanswered questions about this form of social organization.[9] Further study and experiment are needed in various "mega-family" structures. The religious community has long been one such experiment in social arrangement. What it must do now is broaden its social base for experimenting.

My suggestions in this book will probably lead to a charge that I am advocating a change of the religious order into a secular institute. I reject that charge. I am not changing one into the other; I am erasing the line between them. A distinction between people who live in community and those who do not is no longer meaningful. Everyone needs to live in a community, but no one should live in *one* community. The outer things that used to distinguish the religious order are rapidly disappearing, but the secular institute as it has grown up in Catholicism does not offer an adequate model to follow. The words "religious institute" and "secular institute" are misleading terms for what each is trying to be and to accomplish. The new meanings of religion and community that have been previously discussed make the distinction between religious and secular institutes obsolete. The real distinction will pertain to the forms of community that a person prefers and the relation that the person has to the organization of the larger movement.

The more valid objection that might be raised against these proposals is that I am really talking not about the religious order but about the Catholic church and its parishes. A community of men and women who love, live, pray and work together is supposedly what the local parish is. If the reforms suggested here were implemented, it would be debatable whether one should say that the religious order had become the lively parish center or that the parish had absorbed the people who were formerly a religious order.

It would seem logical to hope, therefore, that attempts to

[9] See Bruno Bettelheim, *Children of the Dream* (New York, 1969).

revitalize parish life will converge with similar attempts in religious orders. Unfortunately, the parish is as unbending as the religious order, particularly in its concept of ministry. There is not much indication that the parish is going to uproot itself from the real estate of church and rectory. There is one thing, however, that may bring about a pressure for change. The parish has often been held together by its support of the parochial school. As the parochial school disappears there is a golden opportunity to let the convent and rectory disappear with it. Old churches in the midst of cities might be kept if only for civic tradition. The building of ugly box-like structures in suburbia seems not only unnecessary but dysfunctional. If the church begins to gather its communities wherever and whenever conditions allow, a more precarious but vital existence would probably ensue.

Church authorities should be aware that as new communities spring up, a new form of ministry will come with them. Some of the younger clergy will leave existing church establishments to join these communities. If there are no ordained priests available, other men and women will become the priestly leaders of their communities. At present the situation still looks very clear cut as to which are sacramental and official actions and which are not. Almost certainly, however, the situation is going to become blurred. I should like to make clear that I am not advocating such a blurring. I think that it would be preferable to have existing parish and clergy work with the religious movements now emerging. Roman Catholicism is somewhat precariously held together today with a belief in the necessity of a hierarchy and ordained priesthood. If that belief should all of a sudden crumble, a period of chaos could follow. The fact remains that no one is going to stand still, and advocates of change do not bear all the responsibility for the chaos which may come. Catholicism cannot operate as a closed system any more with the leaders enjoining the members to be obedient to holy mother church. Many of the people who feel that they are being loyal to their Catholic tradition will have no part of the Sunday mass syndrome.

Unless the Catholic church can get its priests out among communities or, better still, ordain its priests within these communities, it is in for some dark days. If the church could trust that the Spirit is working among all people and that new communities are a continuation of what the parish was in another era, the church might find a way through the perilous years ahead. Andrew Greeley has written: "If one is to understand the power and the wisdom of the "new community," one must look at its finer manifestations. One must witness their joy and the courageous outlook which profound Christian charity, exercised in a small group of people, can generate. And when one has witnessed this, he finds it somewhat easier to be persuaded that the New Community could be, if not *the* answer, at least one very important answer; that indeed it might reveal to us the key to pastoral work in contemporary America."[10]

If one is a Christian, there is a point at which he must trust that in spite of evil the world is good, that in the face of difficulties the human spirit can triumph, and that despite our individual failings, God still works in our world. Not only for religious orders and the Catholic church but for society as a whole, we have never more truly faced the best of times and the worst of times. It is not a time for men who are superficially optimistic but it is a time for men who love life and hope boldly. We need people who have the equilibrium to act in the face of odds against them. The power of new communities is still as small as a hand against the horizon, but the power is growing in the streets. Those who are critical of the sometimes pathetic attempts at new communities will have to come forward with alternatives that are better.

[10] Greeley, *The Crucible of Change*, pp. 95f.